The Revolt Against Change

Trevor Blackwell has taught extensively in adult education and has worked as Research Associate at the Centre for Contemporary Cultural Studies, where he was co-author of *Paper Voices* (1975), a study of the post-war popular press. He currently teaches Sociology at Harlow College.

Jeremy Seabrook is an independent writer and journalist concerned with issues of development, social justice and the environment. His most recent books include *Pioneers of Change* (Zed 1993) and *Victims of Development* (Verso 1993). He currently contributes to *New Statesman and Society*, *Race and Class*, *Third World Resurgence* and the *Pioneer* newspaper in New Delhi.

This is the authors' third book together. Their previous book *A World Still to Win: The Reconstruction of the Post-War Working Class* (Faber 1985), was described by the *Guardian* as 'one of the most important books on working class politics . . . in the last 30 years'.

Trevor Blackwell &
Jeremy Seabrook

THE REVOLT AGAINST
CHANGE

Towards a Conserving
Radicalism

VINTAGE

VINTAGE

20 Vauxhall Bridge Road, London SW1V 2SA

London Melbourne Sydney Auckland Johannesburg
and agencies throughout the world

First published by Vintage 1993

1 3 5 7 9 10 8 6 4 2

Phototypeset by Intype, London
Printed and bound in Great Britain by
Cox & Wyman Ltd, Reading, Berks.

ISBN 0 09 930901 7

CONTENTS

Acknowledgements

We would like to thank all of those people who have contributed in diverse ways to the writing of this book. We are particularly grateful to those who shared their experiences with us at St James's Piccadilly, the Centre for Alternative Technology in Machynlleth, the Centre for the Study of Developing Societies in New Delhi and Indranet in Bombay. Thanks also to Frances Coady for her constant understanding and enthusiasm.

London
January 1993

I

IMMOBILISM

TO WRITE ABOUT change at a time of deep conservatism may seem a foolhardy, even doomed, enterprise.

However, the last two decades have seen a deepening opposition between those who have advocated fundamental change as the only way to avoid the complete collapse of industrial societies, and those who have insisted that the continuing of existing forms of social and economic organisation offer the best, indeed only, hope for humanity. Thus, 'We can't go on like this' confronts 'We can't not go on like this'; and the peculiar tension created determines the atmosphere of immobilism in which we live.

In the same evening's TV viewing, we will watch a film about the burning of the rainforests, or the final extinction of some bright-coloured bird which we scarcely knew existed, or the inexorable advance of the world's deserts, and will feel a sense of profound sadness and loss. At this moment, we know that something has to change. At the same time, we will learn from the news programme that economic growth is gathering momentum once more, and that this will provide us with the necessary resources for our enhanced well-being. We may also see the consequences for a country haunted by economic failure – the refugees in flimsy tents in some windswept sandy no-man's land. We may also be invited to celebrate the arrival of some Japanese manufacturing company, which has chosen our country as its base for operations in Europe. At this point we feel only apprehension at the thought of change, for we know that for us change could mean nothing but the surrender of what we have. Change, for us, can only mean worse.

The contradiction is not new, but it has now been intensi- fied. The end of communism has been used to affirm with an even greater finality the superiority, indeed the inevitability, of the market system. On the other hand, people are more than ever aware of the burden placed upon the planet pre- cisely by the success of the global market economy. But it is as though this contradiction simply hangs in the air, unresolved, unresolvable. The worlds of the two consciousnesses cannot, it seems, be brought together. The economy exists in one real world, and nature exists in another. No wonder we are generally happy to keep them apart in our perception, in spite of the sense of powerlessness which this creates.

It is on this base that the present structure of ideological immobilism and numbness of feeling has been built. And it is in this flimsy but strangely permanent shelter that we must make our lodging, find a kind of home for our wounded consciousness. Living in so insecure a place, how can we begin to ask questions about change? There is nothing like being scared to make people cling to what they've got, and to discourage them from asking awkward questions.

When we began this book, our original plan was to talk to individuals about how their lives had changed, and then to seek to generalise from this: how might political change be brought about? We were driven to do this by a conviction that as with individuals, so with society. We knew that change was essential. That we must change or perish has become an insistent theme in all those agonising discussions about what needs to be done, and how people could be brought to see the necessity for change in a perishing world.

So we talked to people. They spoke to us about their epiphanies, their conversions, their moments of revelation, their changes of heart. They shared with us, sometimes very movingly, their formative private experiences, however public their subsequent expression became.

We were disappointed, however, to find that no prescrip- tions emerged. There were patterns – often determined by a life crisis, loss of a loved one, breakdown of a relationship, illness; but these scarcely constituted models or blue-prints. After all, these are the common experiences of every life, and if for some they yield startling insights into the nature of society, for others they furnish the best reasons for the deepest attachment to the status quo.

It occurred to us that perhaps we were looking in the wrong place. What we required were models for collective, rather than individual change. Perhaps if we spent some time listening to those who had participated in collective activity we would gain some clue as to what needed to be done. People told us what had led them to be Green, or how they had come to join the Socialist Workers' Party; how they had found a place within the women's movement, or how they had come to feel at home in some worshipping community.

This had certainly changed them – only the world remained obdurately the same. They, however, gave us two valuable insights. For their perception of the world had certainly altered, and they had correctly identified that what was needed was to join with other people. What we were left with was a series of inspiring but discrete personal testimonies. Something was lacking. There seemed an unbridgeable gap between the personal transformations and a plausible public project which might appear possible to the cynical, the confused, the uncommitted – to that majority of our fellow citizens who live without social hope.

Above all, we were becoming uneasy about the recurring theme that 'people must change'. We began to wonder if the reason why parties advocating radical change were so unsuccessful was because they were striking against the resistance of people who had changed, who had been compelled to change, too much. The experience of industrialisation had been of driven and relentless change, and continues to be so. Even countries which pride themselves on having reached an advanced stage of development, of being post-industrial, of being 'developed', constantly require accelerating change from their privileged populations.

So why should we expect that exhortations to change will be welcomed by those who have known little else for at least two centuries? In this context, the desire to conserve, to protect, to safeguard, to rescue, to resist becomes the heart of a radical project. A form of conservatism – to be most sharply distinguished from its multitude of imitations, its travesties and caricatures, and scarcely known to those who carry the banners of conservatism in the modern world – becomes indispensable to this work of resistance. This conservatism leads us to the search for all those valuable resources that have been thrown away in the process of eager industrialisation. For the greatest casualties in this version of development have been human, perhaps even more than material, resources.

It may seem a paradox that the only radical politics left to us should be based upon resistance, recuperation and remembering. But in a social and economic system which requires the reverse of all these things, to oppose means to conserve.

But this is not to be an indiscriminate work of conserving. What does not need to be conserved is the one thing that the system holds inviolable, beyond change; and that is the wealth and power of the privileged. For all the upheavals and dispossessings that the people of the world have been forced to undergo serve this fundamentally unchanging, but not unchangeable, stasis.

What needs above all to be changed is the current mix of what can be changed and what cannot be changed; and it is this perception that will liberate us from our present oppressive immobilism. A new way of seeing old things, a different way of seeing the same things – this is the change in perception that alone will open the pathway to action. There is another world, but it is this one.

2

CHANGING

IT IS AXIOMATIC in radical politics that people must change. This demand has usually required a changed perception, an altered awareness, by means of which intolerable injustices could be challenged. The focus of radical politics for a long time returned again and again to the condition of the working class. It was a question of creating a new consciousness, which was indispensable for the collective action needed to bring about change. Consciousness was always a prerequisite. It was not a consciousness of oppression or suffering. They knew that too well already. What was needed was a different sense of the nature of the oppression: that it was not a visitation of God, nor part of the natural order of things, but a human-made burden, which could be laid down, provided that the necessary insight and strength could be drawn together. Action required a sense of the arbitrary nature of these crushing impositions, a relativising of them; this could only come from a sense of hope that some alternative might be possible.

This is why the preaching of socialism, which expressed anger at known wrongs and injuries, and encouraged people to believe that life really could be different, was the one thing that offered hope. It gave a vision of how people's generosity could be articulated to construct a better way of being together, a generosity denied by the society that could employ only competition and selfishness.

The early socialists reached very easily for religious language. Indeed, part of the excitement, even the fervour, of early socialism was that it appeared to offer a joyful secularisation of what had hitherto been confined to the realm of religion. For many centuries the work of transformation had been seen exclusively in religious terms. Socialists naturally spoke of 'the scales falling from their eyes' after they had listened to some wandering socialist speaking under the village cross; their speech was of 'revelations', 'blinding light', 'conversions'. They talked of 'preaching the word, in season and out'. The image of the awakening reflected their own experience. They sang:

> England arise! The long night is over,
> Faint in the east behold the dawn appear;
> Out of your evil dream of toil and sorrow,
> Arise, O England, for the day is here.[1]

Emboldened by their own transformation, they encouraged others to rise up out of the long night of ignorance. Organise, educate, agitate, they inscribed on their banners. How easily these exalted preachings subsided into state education, and with what fateful consequences: the transforming power of the word was readily recuperated into the rote learning that prepared students in the elementary schools to adapt to that station in life to which society was to call them.

Awakening suggested irreversibility, as though people, once awakened, would never need to sleep again. It perhaps underestimated both the stresses of continuing to live within a capitalist society, however altered, and the ability of that society to produce its own soporifics. After all, sleep itself is a great comforter. Oblivion, not knowing, not being aware, not seeing the connections, may be a profoundly seductive option, especially when some of the most frightening nightmares have been banished. Indeed, it seems now that one of our most fundamental rights has become the right not to know. Ignorance, in the sense of a denied knowledge, has become one of the most salient characteristics of an information-rich society. 'I don't want to know', 'I just switch off' – whether that means the TV set or the mind is ambiguous – 'I put it out of my mind', 'I try not to think about it too much', 'I try not to let it get to me'. Perhaps social somnolence best describes this uncertain refuge to which so many flee when faced with the reality of the world. Thus impotence has its own comfort. To sleep, perchance to dream: but nothing is left to chance in this elective twilight. Here, the dreams come packaged and labelled. The internal video machine is permanently set, waiting for the flick of a switch, the blink of an eye.

How different the dreams, how different the awakening from those of William Morris's sleeper in *News from Nowhere*, when he wakes from a dream of Britain transformed into 'a garden, where nothing is wasted', a place of security, peace and plenty. The sleeper describes his feelings:

> I lay in my bed in my house at dingy Hammersmith thinking about it all; and trying to consider if I was overwhelmed by despair at finding I had been dreaming a dream; and strange to say, I found that I was not so despairing.
>
> Or indeed WAS it a dream? . . . All along, though those friends were so real to me, I had been feeling as if I had no business amongst them: as though the time would come when they would reject me, and say . . . 'No, it will not do; you cannot be of us; you belong so entirely to the unhappiness of the past that our happiness even would weary you. Go back again, now you have seen us, and your outward eyes have learned that in spite of all the infallible maxims of your day there is yet a time of rest in store for the world, when mastery has changed into fellowship – but not before. Go back again, then, and while you live you will see around you people engaged in making others live lives which are not their own, while they themselves care nothing for their own real lives – men who hate life though they fear death . . .
>
> Yes, surely! and if others can see it as I have seen it, then it may be called a vision rather than a dream.[2]

To talk about the people being wakened from their sleep has even more poignant echoes now. To sleep in wretchedness and poverty is at best a disturbed and fitful rest, to sleep in the hushed comforts of luxury is a more total slumber, and one from which it is more difficult to awaken. If today's sleepers were aroused, they would scarcely open their eyes to the world depicted in socialist iconography. It is significant that this language of awakening was banished to the social periphery in the Sixties and Seventies, where it became the preoccupation of those groups who needed to articulate their opposition to the dominant values, carried then, paradoxically, by a pacified working class. Thus, the black, women's and gay movements took up the language of 'consciousness-raising', 'liberation', 'becoming aware'. This occurred at the same time as the deepening of a more general torpor.

And yet, such struggles are never truly laid to rest, for that would suggest the sleep of death. How strange that the need for a change of consciousness should once more be at the centre of our lives. The Green movement is now the prime contender in urging the need for change. How precisely its debates, its denunciations, its urgencies, echo those of the early socialists. For they talk of humanity sleepwalking towards extinction, of the need to wake up before it's too late, of the necessity for a shift in consciousness if the planet is to survive. They are, needless to say, accused of preaching doom and gloom, of being apocalyptic, of spreading a message of despair by those who are protecting the innocent sleep of the people. Similarly, the Greens debate how the change is to be brought about: can the people wake up and make change voluntarily before disaster occurs, or must they await the rude cataclysm that will rouse them violently, only to plunge them into a possibly final slumber.

The sleep that inhibits change today is both shallower and deeper than that which held in thrall our working-class grandparents. It is shallower in that we now have greater access to global realities: they stare us in the face through the TV screen. But it is deeper in that it seems to perpetuate the advantages which an elective unknowing brings. It is as though it were a drugged sleep; and any awakening from it would be necessarily more traumatic. Detoxification has never been a very agreeable process. All that was required of our grandparents was that they should become aware of the true causes of their own exploitation, and that they should understand the consequences of permitting it to continue unchallenged. Of their suffering they had no doubt. Our generation has a more difficult transition to make. We must choose to leave the polluted and polluting paradise in which we have been invited to remain, it would seem, for ever. What we must come to know is that the apple, beneath its lustrous cosmetic surface, will not only bring a poisoned knowledge, but is also laced with dangerous pesticides.

Radicals, alongside their demand that people must change, equally strenuously bewail their failure to do so. The explanations during two centuries of industrial development have been variations on a few themes: The time is never ripe. The people have not had long enough fully to comprehend the nature of the system which has them in its grip. People have always been too deferential, too inhibited by a sense of their own inferiority in the presence of their betters, of those set over them in authority. Thus they tugged their forelock to the squire, or they cringed before the mill owner, before whose stern regard they sat in their chapel pew; now they fall into a state of open-mouthed admiration at the conspicuous deployment of wealth by pop stars, celebrities and jet-setters. People have always felt it better to keep on the right side of those, whoever they might be, who were the possessors of wealth and power. Continuing to serve them might cause crumbs from the rich man's table to fall into their hands. The people have never lacked alibis for their reluctance to change.

Such homely excuses have been overtaken by the more sophisticated analysis of false consciousness, perhaps the dominant twentieth-century interpretation of the people's unwillingness to change. They have been deceived. They have been deceived by the yellow press, by the jingoistic propaganda of media barons, by the meretricious glamour of the music-hall – and later, Hollywood – and more more recently by the noisy emanations of a global entertainment industry. The media have now become the object of radical vituperation. Were it not for the sinister influence of the mass circulation dailies, the monopolistic escapism of international TV conglomerates, the systematic dissemination of incoherent trivia, the people would have long ago pierced the veils that shroud their own reality from them.

This radical anger is fuelled by a deep disappointment that the very blessings for which their predecessors struggled have been turned into instruments and forms of unknowing which they could never have anticipated. The efforts to achieve mass literacy, which was seen as the supreme means of delivering people from ignorance, gave them over instead to the pernicious influence of the penny dreadful and the gutter press. Education, which was the object of so much aspiration, and which was to have exercised so profoundly ennobling an influence over the minds of the young, instead merely trained them to operate new machinery. Prosperity, which was to have raised their eyes above the pitiful horizon of blinkered insufficiency, has plunged them rather into the consolations of forgetfulness. Welfare, which was to have ensured security, has actually legitimated the increasing disengagement of people from each other's lives.

Generations of radicals have now spent their best endeavours in devising ever less plausible, but more convoluted, excuses for why the people have failed to change.

In the Nineties, particularly after four successive Conservative victories, those who long for change find themselves close to despair. Anger has given way to sadness and depression. It all seems so hopeless, they say. What do you have to do to convince people, they ask. Those who still identify the possibility of significant change with Labour feel immobilised and impotent. Where is the energy, where is the dynamism in anything Labour can offer? There was a moment when the bringing into government of the institutions of labour appeared to guarantee a role in perpetuity for these social groupings and the alternative aspirations they represented. Now, it has become clear that the institutionalisation of Labour has drawn the sting of opposition. Labour now no longer even pretends to challenge the way things are; its highest ambition is not to attack capitalism, but to manage the economy, which is the only guise in which capitalism appears in current political discourse.

In recent years many of those of us who have thought of ourselves as radicals have found ourselves increasingly reduced to a querulous and grumbling impotence with each succeeding manifestation of social injustice. 'I was appalled to read in the *Guardian* . . .'; 'Isn't it disgusting what is happening in education'; 'I was horrified to hear the effects of health-service reforms'; 'It's a shame to any civilised city that people are sleeping in doorways'. In fact, we have become so accustomed to being upset, disappointed and appalled, that it has become familiar, almost comfortable. There is something almost reassuring about those evenings spent in sympathetic company, where we tell each other that we have kept faith. We have not been seduced, unlike others we could mention. And the reward for our constancy has been a slight overdrinking, perhaps, and overloud indignation, a posture of passionate but inactive radicalism. 'Isn't it awful', is perhaps the most constant phrase in our litany of complaint. This is the counterpart of the apparently immoveable conviction of the people that there is no longer anything to be radical about. We say defiantly, we shall not change in our radicalism, just as long as they do not change in their persistent and immoveable conservatism. What is less easily perceived is the reactive nature of this response. What is harder to understand is to see the connection between these two expressions of immobilism. Beneath this apparent opposition there is a symbiotic and petrified acceptance of the status quo.

How misplaced and one-sided such familiar laments are. To talk about the people's refusal to change has a curious resonance at the end of a period of two hundred years which have seen nothing but incessant, remorseless *change*. If there is one thing which is obvious to anybody it is that the last two centuries have been a period of unprecedented change. It is a commonplace to hear centenarians say to newspaper interviewers that they were born in the age of the carrier's cart, and have lived to see rockets on the moon. At whatever moment we look at people's lives, we find a story of continuous upheaval, of accelerating technological change, of forced adaptation, of the unlearning of old ways of life and the rapid acquisition of new ones. Our life has been repeatedly marked by migrations, wars, unemployment, new patterns of working, altered and strange environments. More recently, having learnt the lessons of industrial society only too well, we are confronted by forms of deindustrialisation that threaten to render all that hard-gained knowledge superfluous. And these have not been merely external changes: they have involved radical reshapings of sensibility, internal upheavals, the reworking of psychic structures. Deep inner violence has been inflicted, in the name of progress, wealth creation, development; in short, of change.

The testimony of all those who have been bent to the forces of industrialism has always focused on change. What could have represented a more total overthrow of established living habits than the killing of the family pig for the last time; the abandoning of the handloom whose rhythms had determined one pace of their lives, the leaving of the cottage, where the fowls would soon fly in through the broken windows? What could have been more traumatic than the journey to the spreading town, where people had to submit to the unfamiliar sounds of the factory hooter and the knocker-up, the more constricting rhythms of the factory machines, which forced them to learn the language of the deaf? Nor were these disruptions final, a once-for-all upheaval in the lives of the people, a necessary prelude to a promised time of permanence and stability. What could have been more upsetting than to live through the demolition of the centres of industry which had briefly seemed to be the very element in which we lived? What could have been more disturbing than the constant experience that new skills so painfully acquired, equally swiftly became outdated, unable to procure the livelihood they had recently seemed to promise. What could be more shocking than to stand in front of the humming manufactory fallen into a tangled ruin of twisted girders and broken brick? How can we argue that we are not redundant when we have been urged to find our sense of value and the meaning of our lives in each new mutation of industrial society? The evictions and expulsions from settled patterns of work also repeat themselves, and we seem to have so few resources to withstand this constant remoulding of our functions.

Nor was it only the material fabric of life that was reworked under these necessities. What could have involved a more complete overthrow of values, than the urgings upon an impoverished generation to scrimp and save, to practise self-denial, frugality and thrift, when they lacked the basic wherewithal even to furnish their families with the barest requirements, when the next generation would be exhorted to extremes of prodigality, to spend and to waste, where yesterday's reckless spendthrift is transformed into today's model consumer? Who can measure the confusion and sadness of those who had been brought up to believe that theirs were enduring and unchanging values, only to see such precious wisdom cast off and ridiculed by their own children, inhabited by the urgencies of the next phase of industrial development?

It is fitting that the young become the bearers of such changes, for the promise of stability and security are always in the future. We have been reconciled to the loss of our place in industrial manufacture with the assurance that this old-fashioned superseded activity would be followed by 'real jobs', by permanent and prosperous employment in the new service sector. Within less than a decade the excitement of these changes has been replaced by a bitter recognition that if there is one thing we can be sure of, it is that there will be neither permanence nor security in a world dedicated to accelerating and uncontrollable change, to which there is to be never again any alternative.

If people do not rush to embrace the benign changes pressed upon them by those arguing for radical political change, is it not because they have been compelled to accept so many external visitations, so many transformations which they have been powerless to influence? For change, whatever advantages it may have brought, has also been associated with a sense of loss: the loss of control over the provision of their own food (perhaps the most basic of losses), loss of the ability to vary the rhythms of their working day, loss of closeness with kindred and neighbourhood, a loss of self-reliance, a loss of understanding of the forces shaping their lives. How sad that the advocates of radical change have been unable to perceive and to feel for themselves the abiding sense of loss that unceasing change has brought to the experience of the very people whom they claim to cherish. How sad that they have been able to offer only the thinnest vision of an uncharted future, without even the consolations made available within the existing system.

It should scarcely surprise us if such driven and violent changes call forth the desire to resist. Resistance to change is usually interpreted as a form of conservatism, indeed, perhaps as its most fundamental characteristic. What is less frequently observed is that resistance to change in a world of feverish turbulence and imposed instability, can equally well form the roots of an energising and transforming radicalism.

Resistance to changes imposed is itself always shifting and ambiguous. When William Cobbett regretted the passing of an age of rural sufficiency, he was articulating a widespread sense that improvements in agriculture had at the same time undermined the people's capacity for self-reliance. Whether his response to change was as conservative as was then assumed, we may now question, particularly in the light of contemporary Third World critiques which see the same process of dispossession today, and which argue that forms of development in the name of agricultural productivity and enhanced yields do not necessarily benefit the people, especially those farmers forced off the land. On Cobbett's rural ride between Winchester and Burghclere, he paused at

the little village of Stoke-Charity, the name of which seems to indicate, that its rents formerly belonged wholly to the poor and indigent part of the community. It is near to Winchester, that grand scene of ancient learning, piety and munificence. Be this as it may, the parish formerly contained ten farms, and it now contains but two, which are owned by Mr Hinton Bailey and his nephew, and therefore, which may probably become one. There used to be ten well-fed families in this parish, at any rate: these, taking five to a family, made fifty well-fed people. And now, all are half-starved, except the curate and the two families. The blame is not the landowner's; it is nobody's; it is due to the infernal funding and taxing system, which of necessity drives property into large masses in order to save itself; which crushes little proprietors down into labourers; and which presses them down in that state, there takes their wages from them and makes them paupers, their share of food and raiment being taken away to support debt and dead-weight and army and all the rest of the enormous expenses, which are required to sustain this intolerable system. Those, therefore, are fools or hypocrites, who affect to wish to better the lot of the poor labourers and manufacturers, while they, at the same time, either actively or passively, uphold the system which is the manifest cause of it.[3]

Similarly, when the Luddites were seen as dangerous wreckers, was it because they were seeking violently to destroy new technology, or because they were seeking to protect known and established livelihoods; and is such resistance conservative or, particularly in a world which systematically disemploys people without offering them any function elsewhere, radical? Even Chartism, seen as the most radical movement of early industrial society, had its conservative aspects, in so far as part of its ambition was to challenge the imperatives of industrialisation, and to create those forms of rural self-sufficiency of which earlier ages had often dreamed. Chartism foreshadows some of the more far-reaching alternatives proposed today by those who similarly question the need to surrender every last vestige of autonomy before the imperative of universal industrialism, and who similarly see our best hope in the blending of self-reliance with disengagement from the industrialised answering of human need.

Chartism seriously envisaged a reversal or dismantling of industrial society. After the defeat of Chartism, opposition became focused upon demands for higher rewards for accepting the necessity for change. Much of what passed for socialism effectively said 'If you want us to go along with this, you'll have to make it worth our while.' This was sometimes glorified as the struggle at the point of production, but any serious alternatives to such bargaining were banished to the realm of dreams, of utopias, of visions. The blood-curdling radicalism of Marx served, among other things, to conceal the need for the elaboration of true alternatives to the aggressive expansionism of industrial society. Since the revolution envisaged by Marx appeared to pose the most extreme threat that the existing order could imagine, all other more radical projects readily withered in its life-denying shade.

The widespread acceptance by the people that bribes were a tolerable reward for going along with whatever changes industrialism demanded continued to exist alongside more covert resistances. In spite of gaudy promises of future prosperity and well-being, people nonetheless clung to known patterns of work, livelihood and ways of being. In recent years this has shown itself in a reluctance to accept what has been called – tendentiously – deindustrialisation. Even steelmakers and coal-miners have fought to preserve their places of work, once pictured as the most dreadful hellholes devised by an inhuman system to oppress its captive peoples. This, perhaps contrary to common wisdom, says less about people's innate conservatism than about the pain they undergo and sacrifice they have to make in adapting themselves to those sometimes violent changes that sucked them into such forms of employment. Their caution in giving up the familiar for another unknown destination comes from a well-grounded fear that there will be further pain and sacrifice in store, no matter how seductive the colours of the beckoning future.

As the majority of people have become richer, their conservatism has taken a new turn. Above all, people now want to hang on to what they have got. The meaning of post-war prosperity in the Western world is now clear. Gone are the days when it required subtle sociological probing to discover the nature and effects of affluence. It has quite simply tethered people, apparently by indissoluble bonds, and for all time, to the status quo. All our precious freedoms have come to depend absolutely on money, and its continuous flow. This is the true essence of our dependency culture. But the continuous flow of money itself depends absolutely on endless upheaval, change, destabilisation, dissatisfaction, restlessness, novelty and the creation of new ways of answering need. It is a strange form of conservatism that binds us to the very source of our continuing dispossession! The driven turbulence from which we once sought refuge in our conservatism is now the only refuge we have, with all its radical discontinuities and confusions. The circle is closed; we should not find it strange if we can no longer even dream of an alternative, much less formulate one. Thus conservatism and radicalism are locked together in a strange coupling, whose progeny are to be seen in the distortions and diseases of 'advanced' Western society; advanced principally it some-times seems in its capacity for cruelty, violence, addictions and new forms of deprivation and loss. This embrace of change with continuity is what creates the political, social and psychological immobilism of our age. This is why we feel stuck. This is why we can see no way out. This is why we despair.

When we begin to wonder how we could possibly have got into these strange confinements, we remind ourselves of the long years of struggle that were necessary to gain access to a share in the benefits of industrial society. At an earlier period, nothing was given to the people; the era of free offers, gifts and prizes was yet to come. The pain and the heroism that went into the fight for a decent sufficiency for the majority of the people inhibit us from looking too closely at the negative side of these achievements, the darker aspect of the rewards we have won. The Labour movement, with all its sacrifice and suffering, compelled the capitalist system to part with some of its wealth to those who had lived in poverty, but who were indispensable to its amassing of riches. After this epic victory, how easily the Labour movement has been expelled from the system whose workings it had striven so hard to modify. Whereas once only political economists and laissez-faire ideologues had portrayed the Labour move-ment as an obstacle to the wealth-creating capacities of capi-talism (any abridgement of the working day was always represented as leading to the certain ruin of this nation), it is now Labour's sometime natural supporters who have been brought to share this sombre analysis. They too now see Labour as a hindrance, even a threat, to their continuing prosperity.

This has made it far easier for the same system to claim credit as the sole benefactor of the people. Even if, in days of the youthful exuberance of capitalism, some protection of the workers might have been necessary (however strenuously this was denied at the time), such defences of its former victims have long since become redundant, even malign.

If a capitalist society insists that there is now no place for organised labour, given that it has become the universal provider of the people, this is partly because the Labour movement's relationship to the system it sought to modify was always ambiguous. There was a time when the Labour movement struggled and argued and debated over whether what it wanted was something *more* or something *different*. Embodying what some have regarded as a British genius for compromise, Labour decided that it could have both simultaneously. It was felt that winning a greater prosperity for the people would automatically prepare the ground for a transformation of society. They were not wrong: their only mistake was in the nature of the transformation that would be wrought. But while all imagination and effort was concentrated on gaining a larger slice of the cake for the people, no one thought to question its ingredients; it is only when people start dying of consumption that the wholesomeness of the cake becomes a matter of concern.

The ills of capitalism appear to have abated with the spectacular prosperity of the West. All the symptoms of social disorder and dissatisfaction that remain can no longer be associated with so umblemished a system. And yet the ills remain, indeed new ones appear. These can therefore only be attributed to something that defies reform, the malign forces of unregenerate human nature. Had Labour not urged that the removal of poverty, unemployment, insecurity would lead to a life of contentment and satisfaction, of which previous generations could only dream? In the middle years of the twentieth century, the welfare state, Labour's practical embodiment of its own vision, appeared to have abolished the spectres of want and worklessness. The struggle seemed to be over. What need now for Labour? The system could, it seemed, be trusted to maintain us in the state to which we had rather swiftly become accustomed.

With the weakening of traditional resistances to capitalist growth and expansion, some of its traditional evils reappeared, alongside some that were distinctly novel. Not only did poverty and unemployment appear to be indispensable components of the wealth-creation process, but so did rising levels of crime, addiction, fear, isolation and the breakdown of families and neighbourhoods. All this could no longer be so plausibly associated with a system that had showered its benefits upon the people; it had to be externalised. Social ills became a manifestation, not of systemic flaws but of human weakness or wickedness. What more perfect alibi could have been found than to have attributed the causes of all social wrongs to the hidden and unreformable vagaries of the human heart (known only to the all-seeing eye of God), while all good things could equally readily be ascribed to the beneficent, but equally concealed, manipulations of the hidden hand?

There are at least three powerful reasons for not inspecting too closely the nature and source of the fragile privileges which a majority in the rich countries now enjoy. First, we remember how the lives of our grandparents were dedicated to providing us with a better life, and we dare not appear ungrateful for what they bequeathed us. Second, the provisioning by the capitalist system does render lives in many ways more agreeable, especially if a large part of their true costs is not counted – the costs to our own self-reliance and to our social well-being, the costs to the exploited peoples of the world, and the cost to the resource base of the earth. Third, and perhaps the most pressing influence of all is the fact that what we call our high standard of living is envied by people throughout the world, and threatened by their desire to have what we have got.

It may be that the menaced and impermanent feeling of our tainted comforts makes them all the more desirable, and makes it literally unthinkable that we should relinquish any of them. We know that there is a whole world out there, barely contained within the TV screen, waiting to take possession of what we have so recently won, if we should drop our guard for one moment. We sometimes see the dispossessed at even closer quarters. On our long-haul holidays, we cannot fail to become aware of the outstretched hands of destitute children who won't go away. We are reproached by ragged and emaciated bodies sleeping on the streets. If we distrust the over-eager deference and self-effacements of those who silently wait upon us, this is because we know how we would feel if we were in their place; indeed, sometimes we think we can almost remember what it was like to have to efface ourselves. Did not coachloads of young women come up from Wales to dance attendance upon the metropolitan rich, and were we not among them?

Now that we have come to take our rightful place among the metropolitan rich, we discover that there are so many ways in which we could be dispossessed. There is always the possibility of sudden unemployment (any job is a good job in the contemporary division of labour). We may at any time be robbed (is this why crime is a major moral panic of our time?). We are always at risk from accidents, including such phenomena as economic downturns, or political incompetence. Are we not susceptible to the buffetings of economic storms, the earthquakes on the Tokyo or Wall Street Exchanges, the cold winds of competition from newly industrialising countries? In a cosmos bounded by economic necessity, these become the acts of God against which no insurance company will guarantee us.

In the vulnerable enclosures where we live, the last thing we want to hear is the exhortations of those who would propose a new order of social justice. The justifications for privilege are always legion, and we have inherited them from our betters. Similarly the explanations for continuing poverty are equally numerous, and we are even more familiar with those, because we were so lately their victims. What more needs to be said about the vanity and folly of asking for change? Where our grandparents lived in hope of change, we dwell in its shadow, the fear of change.

If we look with such terror at the prospect of change, this is because we have forgotten that earlier hopes of drastic change were conceived by the belief that the continuous upheavals and disruptions of industrialism could be seized by those they affected, taken hold of and transformed. In this way, those who suffered planned to take control of those changes which dominated their lives, and to apply their

20

energies to benign ends. It is easy in retrospect to see their courage and daring as doomed, an enterprise fit only for working museums on the sites of former industrial towns, fit only for the celebrations of labour historians, with their archives and tape-recordings of the last gasps of an industrial working class on its death bed.

3

LOSSES

THE RELENTLESSNESS OF loss through change cannot be overstated, mainly because it has been so consistently denied. Both Right and Left have their own deep reasons for believing in progress; the Right because they have placed their hopes in the perpetually disruptive forces of capitalism, and the Left because the greater that same disruption, the sooner the day of transformation will arrive. Both have therefore been caught up in an unhappy collusion, in denying the actual experiences of the people. 'You can't stand in the way of progress'; 'It's no use clinging to outmoded ways of life'; 'You have to move with the times': is this the popular wisdom of the Right or the Left? The fact that it has become unclear says much about the self-buttressing stasis upon which contemporary politics has constructed its reason for being.

Although politics has banished any discussion of loss, people's experience continues to be marked by an abiding sense of dispossession, and they articulate this in terms of what has been taken away from them. In the early industrial period, their estrangement from the natural world imbued people with a profound regret. In the cities, it took two or three generations before the memories, stories, beliefs, and habits of country life became extinguished. The homeplace for many people remained the village, to which they and their children returned whenever they could, where they had relinquished so many of their kin, and so many archaic practices which they rediscovered with joy at harvest or Maytime or Michaelmas. The rhythms of agricultural life were not entirely drowned by the harsher cadences of machine labour.

A yearning for a more natural way of life showed itself in the persistence of old wives' tales and herbal remedies, of reading tomorrow's weather in the skies, of growing mint and sage in old pots on the most sunless window ledge in the tenement building.

This longing for what was seen as a better way of life showed itself in a distrust of 'shop-bought' food, bread and milk, adulterated flour, or meat from animals that had died of disease. Given the levels of vitiated food at that time, this was not only very good sense, but it also symbolised that most intimate of losses, the surrender of control over providing one's own sustenance. How this is echoed in the contemporary world in those countries rapidly industrialising and compelling people into the same deprivations which we in the West once lamented in vain. We hear this same sadness in the words of a farmer on the island of Langkawi in Malaysia, when he says, 'People who grow their own food have the greatest freedom of all – control over their own lives. If you work for others, you are not free. How is a boy dressed in a uniform behind a counter in a hotel more free than a man who cultivates his own land?' He watches people sell their land and says, 'The last harvest it will ever produce is a pocketful of dollars. After that, nothing. Money makes land barren.'

People sought a partial reclamation of their forfeited freedoms in symbolic gestures towards providing for their own sustenance, even if this meant only keeping a few fowls for eggs, or growing potatoes in the back yard. For some, the allotment became the last reminder of another way of life. Even within living memory, families would spend a day's holiday on the allotment, take a flask of tea and some sandwiches, sit under the pear tree, and gather gooseberries or raspberries for jam, sticks of rhubarb and runner beans. Then there were the excursions into the countryside to go nutting, gleaning in the empty harvest fields, blackberrying, mushrooming in the early August morning before the dew had evaporated from the grass, fishing for trout or bream; the freely available produce of the countryside had supplemented inadequate diets in the early industrial period.

This loss of contact with the resource base of the earth created a crucial shift in the consciousness of people who underwent it with the greatest reluctance. Few at the time recognised the epochal significance of this cultural upheaval. There were, however, some cultural critics who sought to articulate the enormity of the changes that were taking place, not only in the technology of the age, but also in the sensibility of the people. Thomas Carlyle, in *Past and Present*, noted how

> Our old modes of exertion are all discredited, and thrown aside. On every hand, the living artisan is driven from his workshop, to make room for a speedier, inanimate one. The shuttle drops from the fingers of the weaver, and falls into iron fingers that ply it faster . . . For all earthly, and for some unearthly purposes, we have machines and mechanic furtherances; for mincing our cabbages; for casting us into magnetic sleep. We remove mountains, and make seas our smooth highway; nothing can resist us. We war with rude Nature; and, by our resistless engines, come off always victorious, and loaded with spoils.[4]

This can all be seen more clearly now, as more and more of the world's people are forced to abandon ancient ways of living, and take refuge in city slums. The struggle to preserve the rights of forest and indigenous peoples over their environment, which provides them with a livelihood – whether in the Amazon, in Sarawak, in Central America or India – is precisely a resistance to this loss of control over the resource base. In the early industrial period in Britain, there was no one to fight for us as were were dispossessed, evicted, driven out of our modest claims upon common resources. Should this make us less or more sympathetic to the resistance of those who do not wish to follow our example and the form of development it involves? This may be powerless to rekindle memories of struggles that never took place, but it may remind us of those suppressed and distant losses.

Of course it was poverty that drove people into the cities. Most agricultural labourers experienced indigence and underemployment on the edges of overcrowded villages; but they at least retained the knowledge and the ability to fend for themselves by poaching rabbits, deer and game, however severe the penalties when they were caught. Certain competences and expertise that grew out of their direct interaction with the natural world made life more tolerable. They were protected from the furthest rigours of the cash economy.

Once in the manufacturing towns and cities, even a more or less regular wage could scarcely compensate for the imposition of work rhythms which allowed the worker no variety or variation of pace, but demanded a disciplined uniformity. People were drawn increasingly into a more total cash economy, where fewer areas of self-reliance and autonomy could survive, but were replaced by growing dependency on money. In the beginning, this process may feel like a liberation from the stultifying dependencies of rural life: cash in hand gives a sense of power. It is only later, as older ways of answering need are overtaken, that a more balanced assessment is forced upon us. Any feelings of loss are overlaid by the sudden accession of possibilities that money seems to bring with it. How can we listen to still inner voices that whisper of loss in the noisy colour and bustle of the city streets, where everything is on sale?

And these voices are still not heard when people first arrive in the cities of the Third World today. No matter what circumstances of squalor, violence, cruelty people may live through on the streets of Manila or Bombay or São Paulo, the testimony of migrants is always that it is better than where they have come from. What they have experienced is the growing pressure on the countryside to feed urban populations: levels of oppression in the rural areas turn the most rich and fruitful lands into the sites of indigence and deprivation for the workers there. In the city, they see opulence and plenty and another way of life. It takes some time before they realise that they are leaving one form of dispossession only to enter into another. The sense of violent discontinuity is always with them, but it is not the dominant feeling in the beginning. At least in the city you don't starve.

Later the realisation comes that they hate the city; and if only there had been enough to sustain them in the homeplace, that is where they would have stayed. What they are fleeing is not the 'idiocy of rural life', but hunger and poverty in the very place where plenty is created, and from where it is exported. The longing to return, the desire to go home again are not some idle hankerings after a lost paradise, but the growing awareness that their homeplace has been ruined for them by the same processes that will make life harsh and violent in the city.

Time passes, and the regrets intensify. The resentment at the uprooting fades into a resigned longing, a generalised nostalgia, which, as direct contact diminishes, in the end becomes sentimentality.

The idea that industrialisation is an event, a once-and-for-all occurrence, is profoundly mistaken. Industrialisation is a process, ever-continuing and dynamic. Even the most 'developed' countries are far from having become post-industrial, no matter how little manufacture takes place within their borders. For this reason, there is also no end to the losses and to the regrets which come from the perpetual sweeping away of established and rooted ways of life.

Within the rich Western societies, the cities themselves, thought to be the ultimate expression of industrial society, continue to be broken and remade, destroyed and reconstructed. People who had over generations become an urban working class, created within their neighbourhoods havens, retreats, spaces protected against the most invasive necessities of industry. Such security as they found there proved to be illusory and provisional. Within a generation that urban landscape was itself convulsed, and their fragile and imperfect consoling refuges swept away. Places which, in early Victorian England, had been regarded as the most appalling lodgings of which an injured humanity could possibly conceive, nonetheless became an object of bitter regret, as people were forced out of them. When dwellings where people had lived for generations were suddenly discovered to be 'unfit for human habitation', were 'sub-standard', 'devoid of the proper amenities', similar feelings of loss and nostalgia were widely articulated by those whose lives were being conspicuously improved.

Once again, these were drowned out in the collusive fan-fares of Right and Left, who saw only progress in the move-ment of people into new towns or on to new estates. Those who stood confronting the bulldozers, who obstinately refused to move at any price, who said they would rather die than leave the house where those they loved had lived and died, were seen to be standing only in the way of progress as they cried their defiance against cranes and earth-movers.

Yet these people were really only dramatising what became a more pervasive lament. Even those who most joyfully and enthusiastically abandoned the old back-to-backs felt an undertow of sadness, and were compelled to witness the absence of those neighbourly rituals of tending the sick, laying out the dead, caring for the old, keeping an eye on the neglected. They could not deny that people were decreas-ingly able to amuse and entertain one another, to find satisfaction in the local and familiar. So when they came to say – and to be derided for saying it – that there was a time when people knew how to make their own fun, they were in fact acknowledging that the loss of control continued. The answering of need was passing ever more into the macro-economy. The distance between spontaneous singing round a piano in the front parlour and waiting impatiently for the next twenty-million-dollar blockbuster movie to hit the screen, is vast; but it exemplifies all the surrenders of power that have been passed over in silence. There is a world of difference between entertaining one another and being enter-tained, just as there is between providing one's own food and being fed, looking after each other and being looked after. For all these involve a movement from the active to the passive, from the local to the distant, from the self-reliant to the dependent. We know that something has gone deeply wrong when it is left to vast transnational conglomerates to answer the most simple and intimate of our needs.

Needs created by continuous and dispossessing change are immediately answered by the system that has called them into being. If there is an obscure feeling of regret at the passing of the supports and warmth of neighbourhood, if there is an unease over the decay of a wider family life, capitalism will produce its own surrogates, and will indulge our nostalgias with soap operas that will provide us with the illusion that we can have the best of both worlds, past and present. TV reconstructions of the way we were will offer authentic and detailed versions of our past experience, where we can observe as entertainment what were felt to be grave social and psychological dislocations. What an irony that a system which was responsible for suffering and trauma can reprocess its own woundings as a further, second source of profitable enterprise. All the industrial heritage museums invite us to revisit in our imagination the sites where our grandparents gave up their tribute in blood and pain. Do we pass our money over so easily because we are secure in the knowledge that we will be free of such afflictions and demands; and does this in some way blind us to the forms of tribute that the same system exacts from us now? Because we have left cruder forms of exploitation behind, we do not even look for more sophisticated manifestations of expropriation.

Even within the most unambiguous of gains won from a grudging system, there will be always be something which has to be surrendered. The setting up of the welfare state within Western societies has perhaps been the most unequivocal blessing to its poor and vulnerable. Above all, it gave real relief to women, whose labour humanised the cruel exactions of the classic period of industrial life, and they themselves often became the human sacrifices to it, as well as the scapegoats for the humiliations and unfreedoms of men. While women were themselves also victims of the violent and remorseless change, they nevertheless were compelled to assume the role of comforters and consolers.

Women, freed from burdens, were able to turn their energies towards leading their own lives. No longer tied to dutiful but loveless marriages, they could enter into relationships on their own terms. Released from the prison of the home, they could discover new skills and capacities within the world of paid work. With what a sense of release they could relinquish the onerous ties of duty towards those with whom they discovered they never had anything in common. They could close their own front door on the elective bondings of the nuclear family with its chosen responsibilities and freedoms.

Who would have doubted that such comfortable arrangements could last for ever? Only those who had understood the inner dynamic of a system whose only consistency lies in its power to disrupt and alter and undermine. There are no settled ways of life. There is no status quo. There is only driven change, what some still endeavour to see as progress, what we are all asked at least to acquiesce in as the workings of necessity.

The breaking of the extended family was not enough. Even its nuclear successor has revealed the same tendency to fly apart, to collapse under the severe pressures upon it. Many women have discovered that it is one thing to be able to walk out of a marriage disfigured by cruelty and violence, and quite another to be held prisoner by poverty shared with two or three children on the wrong end of an unaffordable bus route. It is clearly an escape not to be compelled to spend a lifetime in unwaged drudgery for the sake of ungrateful men, but to work at demeaning labour for a pittance in someone else's enterprise can also be an absence of freedom. Because the nuclear family is such a depleted place, the pressure imposed upon a single relationship is hard to bear. There is no one else to run to, no sympathetic ear, no consoling presence. The couple must be all in all to each other or perish. How people cope with this, their heroic sacrifices and enormous efforts and often doomed struggles to stay together is perhaps the next story to be told in the unfolding of what industrialism does to humanity. All that appears so far is that increasing numbers abandon the effort and find they prefer to be alone. Thus it is that loneliness has become one of the distinguishing characteristics of our crowded, busy, sociable lives.

Perhaps we can already discern the outline of the next phase of the industrial reworking of our humanity. Here, the single individual, that icon of all our strivings, finally stands alone, denuded, robbed of all permanent bonds and connectedness to others, isolated in the mighty presence of a single global system. Freed from all constraints of kinship, liberated from even a memory of rootedness, the individual must now buy in all he or she requires. Is this the ultimate one-to-one relationship that we are all looking for? Is the consummation of our humanity to be found in marriage to a system that alone can provide us with affection, food, sex, consolation, entertainment, distraction, culture, company, friendship, escape, a sense of worth and self-esteem? What we may be sure of is that the market, sensitive, responsive and resourceful, will find its own answer once more to the losses it has created, to the mutilations it has inflicted upon us.

For two hundred years we have watched the direction in which industrial society has been leading us, and this is it. It always has been. There is no mystery in its objective: profit. Profit and loss has a resonance which extends far beyond balance sheets. The real losses have been borne by the people's experience of declining power over their own lives, of being unable to resist the intrusions of economic necessities, of the surrender of the ability to do and make and provide things for themselves. Such losses have been directly converted into the gains of the rich and powerful, their accumulations, their version of wealth. The real losses are externalised by the system, and are felt in the realm of the non-economic, in the social, the psychological and spiritual areas of our lives. This is the true magic of the market, the real trick: what is felt only as shadowy, impalpable (but very real) loss, becomes extremely material when it shows up in the profit side of the ledger. What people find difficult in naming to themselves, the accounting system has no trouble at all in expressing and adding up.

What makes acknowledgement of these felt losses even more difficult is that any, however hesitant, articulation of them is instantly derided as nostalgia, an ignorant hankering for a world that never was. Right and Left join once more in symbiotic denunciation of those who dare to question the official story of unquestioned progress. Those who would seek a more balanced assessment are called hopeless romantics by the realists of the Right, and lovers of poverty by the leaders of the Left. There is no space for 'turning back the clock,' say those whose project can only mark time for ever, changeless in their constant insistence on change. 'We must move with the times'; 'That's the price of progress'; 'Don't dwell in the past'; or, more recently, 'We must keep up to date with the "state of the art", be at the cutting edge of meeting the challenge of the future now'. Nostalgia inspires horror because it suggests that our collective escape from the past might not be the bid for freedom that we imagine. The prohibition of nostalgia prevents us from making a more sensitive and complex judgement upon our own experiences.

This accusation of nostalgia is no manifestation of stern realism, but is an ideological weapon. It is the denial by the upholders of progress that there can be anything wrong with the path which we have followed for 200 years of industrial society. If we are so acutely sensitive to the charge of nostalgia, is this because we cannot bear to entertain the possibility that we might have made a mistake, and not a small one that can be easily rectified, but one of such epic magnitude that we must allow the consequences their fullest expression in the world, even if they should damn us to extinction.

It is right that anyone who seeks to evaluate the past should be wary of the treacherous power of nostalgia. Whatever has happened is safe, because it is finished, and is secure against the uncertainties of what is happening now, and of what may happen in the future. Because we have survived the past, we are no longer at the mercy of its events. It can easily comfort us; it is known, familiar. Its solidity acts as a foil against the impalpability of the here and now. Raymond Williams was surely right to warn, in *The Country and the City*, against seeking settled, organic, harmonious ways of life in the past. 'It is clear, of course, as this journey in time is taken, that something more than ordinary arithmetic and something more, evidently, than ordinary history, is in question. Against sentimental and intellectualised accounts of an unlocalised "old England", we need, evidently, the sharpest scepticism.'

This more scholarly view has its counterpart in the easy ridicule of those who scorn memories of summers that were always warm, the good old days when a shilling really was a shilling and you could leave your front door open day and night. A scepticism, however, that can be a useful corrective at one time, can also serve as an aid to illusion at another. In our time, such is our need to feel that we are going somewhere, that the form of development which hurtles us to a benign destination called the future is providential, that we cannot concede that anything swept away in its majestic advance may possibly be of value. Anyone who yearns for what is past beyond recall can only be caught up in some infantile fixation, suffering from a disorder which renders him or her unfit to live in the present.

And indeed, one of the real difficulties in making an assessment of the past stems from the fact that the childhood of all of us is located there, with all its intensities and its boundedness, its continuing spell over our feelings and memories. Whatever dangers might lurk in this longing for an irrecoverable past, they are as nothing compared to that morbid desire for the future which characterises our contemporary culture. As we fall deeper into debt, as we use up the sustenance of our own children, as we consume tomorrow's necessities today, as we sacrifice security of the future for the caprice of the present, nostalgia is scarcely a problem. Indeed, it could be argued that a sober, rational, radical nostalgia might be the most valuable counterweight available to our infatuation with a future which seems certain to bring only impoverishment, hunger and loss to a majority of humankind.

The value of a radical nostalgia might be exemplified in the way in which we view the lives of tribal and indigenous societies in the modern world. Much has been written in recent years in defence of the right of the Yanomami Indians in the Amazon, the Penan of Sarawak, the Lumad of the Philippines to maintain their traditional ways of life. This has been seen as a human-rights issue. What has been less clearly articulated is what we could learn from them, the virtues of not taking more from the resource base of the earth than they put back into it, of harvesting and using its riches in renewable forms. Is not the continued existence of the cultures of indigenous peoples an expression of our commitment to pluralism and diversity in the world?

There are two levels at which the sincerity of our concern

for such people might be questioned. The first is that, however noble our devotion to their self-determination, our devotion to a market economy which is invading and destroying these life patterns, is even greater. Secondly, we have learned to speak a language of 'sustainability', but scarcely to practise it. If we were serious about such a fine concept, we would pay careful attention to the values and beliefs of tribal and indigenous societies, in order to learn from them the principles which have permitted them to survive for millennia.

There can of course be no space for such wild nostalgias in our tidy scheme of things. Traditional, archaic, doomed societies possess vital clues for our own possible survival; yet we see them become extinct, because our fear of nostalgia forbids us to do what is necessary. What is required, of course, is not that we should imitate the details of their way of life – clearly an impossibility, when they are finding it so difficult to maintain this themselves – but that we should pay attention to the underlying principles of sufficiency and careful husbandry and conviviality which have enabled them to survive until assaulted by the superior forces of the market economy.

If our view of other contemporary societies is so limited that we are unable to salvage from them anything of worth, what chance do we have of retrieving anything of value from our own past, over which permanent funerary rites are celebrated?

It is clear that change and continuity are both more complex than they might appear, and the relationship between them more subtle than we might have anticipated. Indeed, it would be the height of political wisdom to be able to distinguish clearly between them, and to analyse how they transform themselves constantly into each other.

4

FALSE ECONOMY

IT IS SIGNIFICANT that although public debate banishes any discussion of loss, it is only too willing to measure 'losses' in financial terms. This is because true loss occurs overwhelmingly, not in those enterprises that go bankrupt, not in balance sheets and company accounts, but in the vast unquantified area of everyday human relationships, social intercourse and personal experience. Because these social costs are incurred in an area traditionally regarded as beyond monetary transactions, they are seen as disconnected from the operations of the economy.

This is one reason why economics is always ideological. It claims to limit itself solely to the practical daily realities of producing, buying and selling; but its dominion has been extended to encompass almost every aspect of human experience. What is not 'economic', that is, that which cannot be turned to profit in one way or another, increasingly ceases to exist in the rich Western societies. In this process, economics imposes a violence upon human beings that is not very different from any totalising creed with its revelations, prescriptions and exclusions.

In the early industrial period, Friedrich Engels saw how what was then regarded as economic necessity destroyed people's lives.

> When one individual inflicts bodily injury upon another, such injury that death results, we call the deed manslaughter; when the assailant knew in advance that the injury would be fatal, we call his deed murder. But when society places hundreds of

proletarians in such a position that they inevitably meet a too early and an unnatural death, one which is quite as much a death by violence as that by the sword or bullet; when it deprives thousands of the necessaries of life, places them under conditions in which they cannot live – forces them, through the strong arm of the law, to remain in such conditions until that death comes which is the inevitable consequence – knows that these thousands of victims must perish, and yet permits these conditions to remain, its deed is murder just as surely as the deed of a single individual; disguised, malicious murder, murder against which none can defend himself, which does not seem what it is, because no man sees the murderer, because the death of the victims seems a natural one, since the offence is more one of omission than of commission. But murder it remains.[5]

Economic forces are mysteriously depersonalised, anonymous, even though both their beneficiaries and their victims are satisfyingly human. This provides alibis for those advantaged by economic necessity; while those who suffer must take responsibility for what is happening to them. There are no excuses for victims. Because the rich are happy to take responsibility for outcomes which favour them, they are insistent that the poor accept the blame for their own impoverishment; which is why there is so much energy expended on explaining the moral inferiority of the poor. Words like undeserving, feckless, irresponsible may have become less prominent, but the judgements have not changed. The rich must be praised and the poor condemned for their participation and respective roles in a system which is a reflection of the natural order of things. It is one of the doctrinal mysteries of wealth creation that an impersonal and unappealable economic system nevertheless so readily generates moral approval and moral opprobrium.

When Engels chronicled the murderous effects of this anonymous system, it was still at a rudimentary stage of development. At that time, it imposed suffering through labour, privation and insufficiency. As industrial society has developed, its power and dominion have extended and deepened. In our time, the workplace is no longer the sole, or even the principal, site of its operations. Indeed, it is not merely our labour that has been confiscated for alien purposes (indeed, a conspicuous absence of function is one of the main characteristics of many people in the rich Western societies), but growing areas of our autonomy, our capacity for self-reliance, our independence and creativity, have been appropriated, only to be turned into commodities and sold back to us. The dreadful secret of capitalist success is that nothing in our human experience is proof against its incursions.

If the people of the West are constantly expressing their need for more, their dependency upon rising income and purchasing power, this is not because they are greedy, but because the inexhaustible rapaciousness of the capitalist system is working and speaking through them. It is not a moral quality – avarice or cupidity or selfishness – that appears to create such a happy convergence between what people want and what the system demands; it is our inability to resist the endless predations upon us, and our desperate need to retrieve at least part of, or a semblance of, what has been stolen from us. When Engels was writing, at least it was possible to perceive the nature and source of what was being taken from people, but as the levels at which the system works upon us have deepened, it becomes progressively more difficult to name and to combat the process of expropriation that continues and intensifies.

We are here at the heart of the only continuity known to a system that demands ceaseless change in the monstrous pursuit of its self-expansion. There is no end to its dispossessings.

What other mysterious source of 'productivity' could exist in the world than the bottomless and formless desire of human beings for what they can, as well as what they cannot, have? The cunning crafting into marketable things of all that is impalpable, of all the yearnings and aching emptinesses that accompany our human lives, has been the central activity of two centuries of industrial endeavour. Lear was right, when he admonished the undemanding Cordelia, 'Nothing will come of nothing. Ask again.' The fabulous productivity that has created the richest societies in the world equally requires something substantial to feed upon. Human beings are mined and undermined for their riches, just as the natural world has been mined and undermined for its treasures. And it is the fusion of these resources that has been the source of Western wealth. All human powers and abilities to do and create and make things for themselves and each other have been replaced by the capacity of money to buy in whatever they find needful.

Perhaps this is why so many industrial struggles over money miss the point, no matter how bloody, cruel and necessary these may have been in their context. Such struggles must always remain symbolic of a far deeper dynamic that is working away, not only in the remote places of the earth, but also in the most intimate places of our humanity. Capitalism prises away, both from nature and humanity, those resources that will be shaped into commodities, upon which we shall come to depend for our sustenance.

The real costs of all this have never appeared in any industrial accounting system, because they cannot be measured there. These are merely some of the losses that are rigorously excluded from balance sheets, for if they were to appear there, all such balance sheets would plunge into the deepest red.

When these costs are elided, 'externalised', they do not disappear from people's lives, but the connection between personal losses and economic gains becomes more difficult to perceive. In the early industrial period, in spite of the daily injuries which capitalism inflicted upon the people, they nevertheless found it difficult to understand precisely how capitalism was the agent of their dispossession. How much more difficult it becomes to make these connections when we see the self-transformation of capitalism in its Western heartland. Now that capitalism is perceived as the universal provider, it has become a kind of blasphemy to question its total beneficence. Now that such a noble system has been brought to high perfection, the only flaw in the world is revealed as a defective humanity. This means that people alone are responsible for any sufferings they incur: poverty, unemployment, any other social evils are all reflections of human weakness, of a fallible human nature that is simply not perfectible.

That people can be persuaded to take personal responsibility for socially determined wrongs is perhaps the highest achievement of a strangely advanced capitalism; advanced principally in its resourcefulness in making profit out of the very losses and sufferings it has itself inflicted. The pain and disturbance of people's lives, all their dissatisfactions, unanswered needs and violent compulsions have been welcomed into a marketplace that provides a specific for each of them. In an earlier age, these remedies may have taken the form of laudanum, opium, the dram shop or the gin palace. In more recent times, there has been an explosion of the ways in which capitalism can heal its own woundings. It seems the need for distraction and escape and consolation has become immeasurably greater with the progress of the system, so that now whole industries offer a world of leisure, repose, escape, entertainment, therapy, stimulation, pacification.

The losses inflicted upon humanity for the sake of profit themselves become a source of enhanced gain to a system that alone knows how to respond to them. (And it is a system. Those who object to the word 'system' speak as though it were organic and spontaneous; like apple blossom. It is a system: ordered, predictable, devoted to a systematic singularity of purpose.) How circular and inescapable it all seems. The only remedy must be sought in an exacerbation of the sickness. Why should such benign arrangements ever be disturbed? The circle is closed, and we must live in it for ever.

There are many ways of suppressing these difficult discussions. We have already noted how the accusation of nostalgia so easily prohibits serious examination of the past. Even more fundamentally, as we shall see, the axiom that human nature cannot be changed serves as a convenient anchorage for the continuity of a system that also involves unceasing change. It is under this fatalistic sign that the constant losses demanded by an unchanging profit motive have been made acceptable; so that when each new forfeit is visited upon the people, their protest is silenced by the invocation of the spectre of human nature. If people must abandon old skills, they are told that they have to live in a competitive society, and that such a society is grounded on the unalterable realities of human nature. If people protest that current levels of crime and social disorder are intolerable, they are referred again to that human nature of which the statistics are simply a melancholy expression. And they will be asked whether they seriously expect mere politicians to legislate against human nature.

5

NORTH AND SOUTH

JUST AS IN the countries of the rich North it has become
unthinkable to talk about change (apart from that borne by
the necessary deepening of industrialisation: consider Clin-
ton's declaration, at the beginning of his presidency, that 'we
must make change our friend'), so in the poor countries of
the world, the official rhetoric is about little else.

In this way, no politician in a country like India will set
forward a prospectus defending the status quo. It is axiomatic
that monstrous social injustice, poverty, hunger and disease
are the objects of a crusading mission. The extirpation of
these things must be on the banners of all who have any
hope of being taken seriously.

We see here the mirror image of the preoccupations of the
North: for the changes being offered to the South are now
almost entirely changes which tend in the direction of the
Northern developmental model; and since that has, at its
heart, the exacerbation of inequalities, the creation of poverties (some of them strange and unfamiliar, it is true, and
which may not immediately appear for what they are to the
bonded labourer or the subsistence farmer on the degraded
soils of Orissa or Bihar), the one sure outcome is continuity
in oppression and poverty for the great majority of the people
of India, or Brazil or wherever it may be.

This is how the rhetoric of a North committed to continuity, and of a South committed to change, actually mesh
into forms of immobilism that both legitimise and justify the
maintenance of the existing order: neither will produce the
developments which they promise to their peoples; yet

continuity (of fundamental inequalities) within constant change (new ways of perpetuating these fundamental inequalities) will certainly be the experience of both. Those who will be satisfied with such an outcome are the elites of both North and South, who alone have something to gain from preserving the present social and economic order.

We who have lived through many generations of industrial experience now find it difficult to recapture the intensity with which people felt the initial process of industrialisation. So much has happened to clutter memory and block the transmission of what might have been remembered. We pore in vain over the classic texts of the nineteenth-century observers and commentators, trying to read between the lines of their spare evocations, to guess at what was going on in the minds of the people who are seen as the victims of these processes. Engels, Henry Mayhew, Charles Booth all came close to the sites of desolation of the early industrial landscape. We see the figures they vividly portrayed, sometimes we catch the smells and hear the accents; but how elusive the consciousness and the feelings of these figures remain.

Engels, writing of the 'surplus population' in *The Condition of the English Working Class* in 1844, describes how

> Along the great highways leading into the cities, on which there is a great deal of waggon-traffic, a large number of people may be seen with small carts, gathering fresh horse-dung at the risk of their lives among the passing coaches and omnibuses . . . Happy are such of the 'surplus' as can obtain a push-cart and go about with it. Happier still those to whom it is vouchsafed to possess an ass in addition to the cart . . . Most of the 'surplus' betake themselves to huckstering. On Saturday afternoons, especially, when the whole working population is on the streets, the crowd who live from huckstering and peddling may be seen. Shoe and corset laces, braces, twine, cakes, oranges, every kind of small articles are offered by men, women and children; and at other times also, such peddlers are always to be seen standing at the street corners, or going about with cakes and ginger beer or nettle beer. Matches and such things, sealing-wax, and patent mixtures for lighting fires are further resources of such vendors.[6]

41

Similarly, Mayhew in *London Labour and London Poor*, describes the Saturday-night markets in London:

> The scene in these parts has more the character of a fair than a market. There are hundreds of stalls, and every stall has its one or two lights; either it is illuminated by the intense white light of the new self-generating gas-lamp, or else it is brightened up by the red smoky flare of the old-fashioned grease-lamp . . . Here is a stall glittering with new tin saucepans; there another, bright with its blue and yellow crockery, sparkling with white glass. Now you come to a row of old shoes arranged along the pavement; now to a stand of gaudy tea-trays; then to a shop with red handkerchiefs and blue-checked shirts fluttering backwards and forwards.[7]

In spite of the vigour and energy of these evocations, they remain distant from us, picturesque even. Is it possible that the people who walk through these scenes could be people like us? How can we make the leap of imagination that would allow us to see the world through their eyes?

The truth is that the actuality of these images has not vanished from the world; nor do we need to make any heroic acts of recollection. We may trace our steps with school-children around the sanitised sites of heritage museums and working factories, but we shall learn very little. What we need to do is to look attentively at those who every day are subject to the very same changes that our own forebears knew, changes which still form the topics of theoretical disputes about standards of living and levels of happiness during the period of early industrialisation. Such people still throng the roads leading into Third World cities; and what they find when they arrive there echoes faithfully the effaced experience of our own people.

For the pressures worldwide are still upon people to leave the countryside and settle in the cities; and those pressures are not so different from those which drove the people into the manufacturing districts of Britain in the early nineteenth-century – 'rationalised' and industrialised agriculture, the concentration of land in ever fewer hands, displacement of agricultural workers by mechanisation, and the growth of population. Many are obliged to find shelter in the slums and shanty towns that inspire in the middle class a distaste and fear similar to those which the slums of London or Manchester once provoked.

In the country, it may, perhaps, be comparatively innoxious to keep a dung-heap adjoining one's dwelling, because the air has free ingress from all sides; but in the midst of a large town, amongst closely built lanes and courts that shut out all movement of the atmosphere, the case is different. All putrefying vegetable and animal substances give off gases decidedly injurious to health, and if these gases have no free way of escape, they inevitably poison the atmosphere. The filth and stagnant pools of the working people's quarters in the great cities have, therefore, the worst effect upon the public health, because they produce precisely those gases which engender disease; so, too, the exhalations from contaminated streams . . . [People] are deprived of all means of cleanliness, of water itself, since pipes are laid only when paid for, and the rivers are so polluted that they are useless for such purposes; they are obliged to throw all offal and garbage, all dirty water, often all disgusting drainage and excrement into the streets being without other means of disposing of them; they are thus compelled to infect the region of their own dwellings.[8]

Engels might well have been writing about Manila in the Philippines in 1992, where people are arriving at the rate of 300,000 a year. One of the most infamous places is Smoky Mountain. This is a vast garbage dump beside the docks, beyond the long-established Tondo slum on the foreshore. Smoky Mountain takes its name from the fact that this extensive hill is constantly smouldering from the subterranean fires that burn at its core. In spite of this, it has become home to thousands of people who have built their houses on areas of garbage that have been flattened; indeed, terraces have been carved into the mounds of compressed rubbish, and some people have planted plantains and flowers in front of their huts.

The area smells of sulphur dioxide, with occasional wafts of salty sea air and the smell of fish. The rainwater at the beginning of the wet season churns the dust into a yellowish paste, with rivulets of rust from the metal walls and fraying sides of the huts. The huts are made of panels of corrugated metal, plywood, rattan, bamboo, and some have polythene or nipa roofs. Many of the structures have been pieced together with considerable skill, even artistry.

There is no electricity, no running water. Most of the women cook on open fires of wood which they pick out of the garbage. Those who are slightly better off buy cylinders of gas. The physical aspect of the people working on the dark mountain in the rain is shocking: the coils of smoke unwind around them, and they cover their heads with sacking; they fight for access to each new truckload of rubbish. There is a complex division of labour, as the workers each specialise in one commodity – glass, plastic, paper, metal. Here, it seems, nothing is thrown away but the people.

If the squalors of Victorian London are recreated in Smoky Mountain, its luxurious excesses have their counterpart in the lives of Manila's rich. A few kilometres from Smoky Mountain is the Malacanang Palace, which the Philippine government threw open to the people in order to display the private opulance of the Marcoses during their dictatorship. On show are the ballroom and disco, the private hospital, the famous wardrobe and celebrated shoes, even the battery-operated glass slippers which lit up as Imelda moved, and gave tiny electric shocks to the soles of her feet, which stimulated her to dance the night away. There is a portrait of Imelda as Eve, after Botticelli's *Venus*; her superstar dressing room is intact, with its lights and mirrors, its Adam furniture and its wine decanters filled with perfume, which dispense their contents by the turning of a faucet. Ferdinand's dialysis machine is still in place, as is the chapel, with its glass, icons and statues, brought from all over the world. When Imelda went to Indira Gandhi's funeral, she used the occasion for a little shopping, returning with some chairs of solid silver inlaid with ivory, and some Hindu temple art. There is a whole room devoted to gifts bestowed upon the Marcoses – Cartier clocks, a diamond-studded handglass, Bohemian glass, Wedgwood, Sèvres, all behind bulletproof glass. There are photographs of the Marcoses taken by their friend Gina Lollobrigida, cabinets of medicines, and the secret exit to the vault which was looted when the palace was overrun in 1986.

Such extremes of poverty and wealth were well documented by nineteenth-century observers, but the pictures they have left for the most part fail to reveal what the people felt and thought as they lived through these experiences. Although the texts may be silent, there is no need to remain ignorant of these thoughts and feelings because they too are recreated in the people whose lives occupy the same setting and take place under the same conditions. We can ask the people of Manila how it feels to live like this.

Lino is twenty-one, and has been in Manila for four years. He came from Ozamiz City on Mindanao in the South. He is from a family of twelve, and his father left when Lino was two. He started to earn money when he was nine by selling sweepstake tickets. Then he drove a tricycle rickshaw, as well as selling cigarettes and candies at the cock-fights, which are one of the most common popular entertainments. Later he was a vendor of Juicyfruit and bubble gum. The family lived in a squatter slum. At sixteen, he came to Manila, working as a houseman, cleaning offices and discos for ten pesos a day. He stayed with a cousin, where he had to do all the washing and cleaning for his keep. He was very sad and lonely when he came to the city; but he is now a sacristan in the church. More recently, he has worked as a lift boy in one of the hotels, where he shares a room at 600 pesos a month, and earns fifty pesos a day. He says that a Saudi staying in the hotel wanted sex with him. 'I slapped him and told him I was an elevator boy not a whore boy. He complained about me to the manager. I said to the manager, "This is not part of my duties", and he agreed with me.' Lino says he has a patron in Switzerland. 'His son died, and he said I reminded him of his boy. I'm hoping to get a visa to go over there.'

Nestor, who is in his early thirties, drives a jeepney (a painted jeep taxi). A year ago, his wife went to Japan on a tourist visa. He later discovered she had no intention of coming back. She got a job as a receptionist at a hotel in

Tokyo. At first, she was unhappy, and would call home almost every day. The calls then became fewer. She sent many consumer goods. Now she has not been in touch for six weeks, and Nestor assumes she has found someone else. Many Filipinos in Japan find 'husbands' and stay on. Nestor says, 'The children keep asking me when she's coming back. I'll give her another six months. If she doesn't come back, I'll have to look for another woman, but I don't want to. I love her. She went to Japan for the same reason I came to Manila – for a better life. I came for the bright lights, only nobody told me you can't eat bright lights.'

Mabini Street is the fun quarter of Manila, with its saloons and theatre lounges, its strip shows with girls in red feather boas and fishnets, its antique and curio shops, cosmetic-surgery clinics and clinics for instant diagnosis of sexual diseases, sushi bars and brothels. Leonor is a dancer in a karaoke saloon. She earns 200 pesos a night, and is also pregnant, the worst fate that can befall a showgirl. After the show, there are often men, usually foreign tourists, who hang around. This one was German. He promised to take her home. When he left, the address he had given was false. She sends money home to her family, telling them she is working as a waitress. She can't go home now. She says she has asked God to let the baby die.

Whatever exotic elements there might be in these testimonies, they echo very plainly the sense of upheaval and loss felt by those coming into the towns and cities of early industrial Britain. We need to listen to such people, because so few in the rich North can now articulate the pains and penalties of what industrialisation does to people.

It is not simply a question of taking snapshots in time of similar social and economic situations, and pointing up the parallel. There is a deeper continuity, a more profound connection than the mere scenery which links both our and their experience of capitalist development. For even if we appear to be further down the road, it is still the same road, and what we have in common above all is that it leads to the same goal; and that remains the enrichment of others and the depowerment and dispossession of ourselves. The forms of impoverishment which we see in the South are used to frighten us into accepting the different forms of impoverishment which we must also undergo. 'Development' in our context means simply more or less advanced kinds of deprivation, the most painful of which is that we have been robbed of even the hope of imagining another way of being in the world, another way of answering our common needs. No wonder increases in existing wealth become so important: these have to compensate for all our lost liberties. It is this dynamic of dispossession which produces the fundamental continuity that joins the slum-dweller in Engel's Manchester with the inhabitant of an ample though insecure suburb in any Western country, and with the people ekeing out a living on the slopes of Smoky Mountain. What we all have in common is that something vital has been taken away from us, whether what we lack is bread or shelter or hope or purpose. The only difference between us and them is precisely what is being removed from our control and competence at any one time.

People in the Third World remain in the countryside until life there becomes intolerable. It is only when the woman on the Brazilian plantation, growing pineapples for export which cannot feed her malnourished children, reaches the point of despair that she will leave for São Paulo. It is only when the landless labourer in Bihar can no longer find work for one day in three in the year, that he will leave his family, and seek employment as a rickshaw puller on the streets of Delhi. When they shift to the city, they take with them the memory of how things were before alien pressures forced them to alter settled practice and tradition. It should scarcely astonish us if we hear from them stories that echo the displaced countrypeople of nineteenth-century Britain.

Engels, no apologist for rural life, gives one description of the pre-industrial handloom weavers:

> These weaver families lived in the country, in the neighbour-
> hood of the towns, and could get on fairly well with their
> wages, because the home market was almost the only one,
> and the crushing power of competition that came later, with

the conquest of foreign markets and the extension of trade, did not yet press upon wages ... So it was that the weaver was usually in a position to lay by something, and rent a little piece of land, that he cultivated in his leisure hours ... true he was a bad farmer and managed his land inefficiently, often obtaining but poor crops; nevertheless, he was no proletarian, he had a stake in the country, he was permanently settled, and stood one step higher in society than the English workman of today ... They did not need to overwork; they did no more than they chose to do and yet earned what they needed. They had leisure for healthful work in garden or field, work which, in itself, was recreation for them, and they could take part besides in the recreations and games of their neighbours, and all these games contributed to their physical health and vigour. They were, for the most part, strong, well-built people, in whose physique little or no difference from that of their peasant neighbours was discoverable. Their children grew up in the fresh country air, and if they could help their parents at work, it was only occasionally; while of eight or twelve hours work for them there was no question.[9]

We should not imagine that Engels is documenting an historical curiosity, for people are being displaced, in the same way, for the same reasons, and from the same occupations today.

Raipur, Central India, 1992. A slum settlement in the centre of this fast-growing industrial city. A community of about 500 people, in huts of mud, wood, metal, none higher than about five feet. Families of eight to ten people sleep in one room, with an earth floor, the kitchen separated by a mud wall. The cooking fires fill the huts with choking smoke; there is no ventilation.

Most of the men here are cycle rickshaw drivers. The work of driving is arduous and backbreaking, and rarely yields more than twenty or thirty rupees a day (between forty and sixty pence). There is extreme competition. Most have taken a loan to buy the rickshaw. Many of the vehicles stand idle, a tangle of black-painted metal, with a plastic seat for the passengers, sometimes with a threadbare canopy to protect the occupants from the rain or sun. The only other work open to men is construction; if they are trained masons or carpenters, they may make a better living. Some women also work as construction labourers, others work in small garment or plastics factories, but the majority are domestic servants.

They have been here for twenty-five years. Why did they come from the neighbouring state of Orissa in the Sixties? 'There is no farming there. It was a place of drought. There was no food grain. Traditionally, we were weavers. But because there is weaving by machine now, there is no work for us. There was skill and beauty in what we made. We took pride in it. But if we were to do that now, no one would buy from us, because they do not want traditional cloth; they think our work is old-fashioned. We came from Orissa because the land had become unproductive. There, we were happy. Here we are not happy, but we can eat. Anything is better than hunger, so even if unhappiness is the price you pay, you will pay it. Unhappiness is the price of survival.'

In the same year, the *Economic Times* of India reported that in Patna,

> hundreds of impoverished weavers met at a conference and spoke for thousands of their comrades when they said they could not light up their kitchen hearths four days in a week. In Panipat, ninety-nine per cent of the weavers do not own their own looms and almost the entire industry is in the private sector and non-household units. In Nagpur weavers work twelve hours a day for fourteen rupees (about twenty-five pence), and in all other weaver households in Delhi, Uttar Pradesh, Bihar, Andhra Pradesh and, Orissa, women work all day long on pre- and post-loom processes without any wages at all.[10]

The point is not that the country, the village, was ever the site of an idyllic way of life, but that life there has been rendered unendurable. It is the sense of having been evicted that tempts us to look back and see it as paradise. The truth is, it was better than it became when we were compelled to leave; and that is the lived experience of migrants to the city worldwide. When people in the cities say, 'It may not be very good here, but it is better than where we were', what do they mean? They are saying that the homeplace had become uninhabitable; and the life they would like to have lived there had been taken away from them. When people in the *favelas* (slums) of São Paulo say that they prefer the dangers of crime, violence, unemployment, drugs, the break-up of families to life on the plantation, they are stating the obvious: that anything is better than starvation. Those who would claim that it is the easy life of the city that attracts people are ignorant: far from being easy, life in the city is not secure, decent or even dignified.

Everywhere, people cling to memories of country life, their peasant past, the subsistence farm. This is especially true of countries like India. In the long Bombay mill strike of the early Eighties, even though the mill-workers had led an urban life for two or three generations, they nevertheless returned to the villages, or were sustained by relatives in the countryside, who fed them during the long dispute.

After generations of urban experience in Britain, the memories of the countryside are modified, even as the countryside from which people came is itself changed beyond recognition. The yearning for 'country life' remains. In recent years, these longings have been realised by those privileged enough to buy up small country properties as holiday homes, or those who live in former villages, which have been swallowed up by the expanding cities. With what relish people set about doing up the kind of properties in which their great-grandparents might have lived, cottages without amenities, with no running water, shared lavatories, a single tap in the yard, smoky paraffin lamps or naked gas-jets in the wall.

If the realisation of this ancient dream has now become possible, this is because it takes place, not so much in the actual geographical setting of the village, as in the realm of fantasy. There is no earthly function for these new suburban villagers, who commute daily to town or city. They have neither place nor role in any conceivable rural community. Yet they have arrived. The migrants have returned. This is the hope of Jamaicans, living in draughty multi-occupation in North London, echoing stairwells and condensed breath in the dank interiors. This is the desire of the Turks, as they listen at night to the trams rattling over the cobblestones beside their tenements in rainy North German cities. This is the longing of the Ethiopians with their suitcases under the tightly packed beds in the barrack-like lodgings near Termini station in Rome.

If those who are now in possession of this shadow country life find that the satisfaction of their dreams still eludes them, is this because it is impossible to get away from it all, when the dynamics of industrialisation have penetrated every last nook and cranny, not only of the countryside, but also of the imagination? No wonder the work of renovating and restoring the cottage is so important. It is not only the decayed timbers that must be removed, but also all traces of the dispossessions and evictions inflicted upon those who once lived here. It is an exorcism of past sufferings, to make way, as it turns out, for present pain, in whatever novel forms this may take.

If we are looking for some clue as to why the wealth and good fortune of the West are so often accompanied by violence, unhappiness and dissatisfaction, we may find it in the suppression of the true costs, in the denial of the real losses incurred at an earlier historical period of industrial society, which are still being inflicted on a vast scale all over the world. There is something unbearably poignant in the discontents of the world's rich who appropriate the necessities of the poor without, for all that, seeing their own lives enhanced. However much more money they get, or desire, or think they need, it can never be enough, because the dispossessions they have known occurred in a realm where money has no power. Money cannot measure, nor respond to, nor assuage the feelings of impotence, restlessness, and exclusion that are inseparable from the good life of the West. A system destined for ever to turn everything it touches into monetary values is doomed to leave its people forever unsatisfied.

When we look at the people of Manila or Bombay or any other city, we should see them, perhaps, not as competitors with us for scarce resources, nor as rivals whose needs threaten our unstable well-being, but rather as our own past experience made flesh in the present. They are the reincarnations of past lives we can no longer remember, they are the bearers of a story that is also our story, but a story which we have falsified in the telling. We say to ourselves that what is described to us as our high standard of living is nothing more than our just desserts: 'I've worked damned hard for what I've got'; 'I've slaved my guts out to give my kids a better chance in life'. We see what we have as a reward for past privations, and for our individual effort. Secure in earned privilege, we survey the world and find ample reason why the poor of the earth do not, indeed should not, share our riches: 'If they worked as hard as we had, they'd be where we are now'; 'If they weren't so lazy, if they got off their arses and did a proper day's work . . .'; 'All this aid we give them, and what do they with it?'

However, if hard work were a sure guarantee of material prosperity, then there is no doubt that the meanest pavement-dweller in Calcutta or Lima would be among the richest people in the world. The barefoot child who sets out on an eighteen-hour workday before dawn with a hessian sack over his shoulder, to forage for scrap paper, waste metal or fragments of broken glass, and who will bring the result of his day's labour to the middleman's scales late in the evening – why is he poor? The woman who walks ten kilometres in search of a pitcher of water and enough fuel to cook an inadequate portion of food for her family – why has her labour not been rewarded with even enough to live on? The woman working in the sub-contracted sweatshop providing the finished product for Hindustan Lever, who earns less than ten rupees for her ten-hour day – if she is unable to make a living wage, what would we advise her to do?

These are not rhetorical questions. We should know the answer to them, since they are questions which our own families had to ask themselves not long ago. The women who sighed over the endless tubs of washing, the men who worked long dangerous hours in badly maintained mineshafts or ill-protected forges, the people who left their limbs on military or industrial battlefields – what did they say to themselves, how did they answer? They knew that prosperity was not necessarily the result of hard work, though they did not cease to work hard for all that. What comfort is it to those long-dead toilers that we seize so much of the world's substance for our own enjoyment? And how does it help those who labour just as they do in Manila or Bombay? And why is this still apparently not enough for our sustenance?

Do the suppressions in our own story help us to understand why we feel so disturbed when the people of the *barrios* and the *barangays*, the slums of Latin America and the Philippines, protest against those developments in industrial society which rob them of control over their own lives? We feel uneasy, because they are articulating protests that were once ours also, before we came to our senses, those senses that are so clouded and troubled now. When we see images of people coming out of the slums to demonstrate on the streets of Seoul or Karachi, and the military turn their guns upon them or hose them with water cannon; when we see groups of ragged tribals and forest-dwellers camped out the High Court building in Kuala Lumpur or in front of the Environment Ministry in Brasilia, we are dimly aware that here are the world's true conservatives. Their purpose is to conserve known, valued and comprehensible patterns of living. They make their stand against the reckless sweeping away of traditional harvesting and husbandry, of millennial management of resources, of ways of co-operating and pooling resources, of benign interdependency between themselves and the rest of creation. They want, above all, to keep things as they are, or at least to slow the rate of destruction of the way things have been.

But war has been declared upon these heretics by the merchants of more, by the missionaries of eternal expansion. In the actions of these dissidents, who have been pushed aside by the bulldozers and earth-movers of prospectors and entrepreneurs, we may find the true roots of conservatism, a conservatism which resists the gratuitous transformation, the unnecessary changes that would take from us what we have in order to offer us what we may no longer have without money.

6

CONSERVATISM AND RADICALISM

JUST AS WE see our own past mirrored in a Third World present, so we can see their resistance to industrialisation prefigured in the opposition of many in Britain in the early nineteenth century. Such resistance was often expressed as a form of conservatism – a desire to hold on to existing ways of life, to the known and familiar. Those who questioned the purpose and direction of industrial society then were scorned as old-fashioned, as enemies of progress. If they became more active in their refusal to move with the times, they were called wreckers, machine-breakers, subversives. That such rebellious and mutinous spirits were so close to conservatives perhaps suggests something of the complexities of political analysis that have been squeezed out of more recent discussions on what it might mean to be conservative, and what it might mean to be radical.

As industrial society has mutated, so the forms of conservatism which have sought to inhibit its imperatives have also developed. Whereas an agrarian way of living served as a focus for conservative feelings in the early industrial period, this was no longer available to subsequent generations, who nevertheless sought to resist further change. As industrial society became more incontestably established and more difficult to challenge on the grounds of an older moral economy, so the desire to conserve attached itself to the new ways of living that had evolved within industrialism, and which, with time, appeared to offer some stability and continuity. In this way, machines that had once been the object of the destructive fury of the workers, at a later date became the guarantors of continued employment of the skills they had developed, and as such, objects of some solicitude, even affection, as compared to a new generation of machinery that threatened to deskill them once again.

It comes as no surprise that conservative sentiments should have been enlisted in common-sense, down-to-earth objections to hare-brained or utopian schemes for changing the world. Have we not been through enough upheavals and alterations and disturbances without deliberately adding to them? Caution, scepticism, mistrust of the unfamiliar – how these popular values nourished the arguments of those who preached the virtues of continuity and stability throughout the discontinuities and instabilities of the nineteenth century!

It is a central irony of the way things work that capitalism has always promised an elusive stability to the people. It always requires an acceptance of one more set of changes in order to attain a security that will endure. There is always only one more obstacle on the path to this happy state of peace and prosperity that has been eternally promised. Thus the people were summoned to leave behind the limited horizons of field and farmyard for the broader perspectives of city life; they were offered war to end all wars; they were promised a land fit for heroes; they were told that if they would make yet one more adjustment to the demands of technological change, all their fortunes would be made. And throughout there has been the recurring final demand that if only they would tighten their belts, make one more sacrifice, better times would surely come. It is hard enough to keep up with the continuous change which simple progress demands of us, without having to listen to soap-box orators who want us to turn our world upside down of our own free will, for God knows what uncertain benefits in some distant future. Is not the struggle to survive, the effort to get by, sufficient, without chasing after utopian dreams, or worse, blue-prints for the reconstruction of humanity? Yet does not capitalism hold its own version of utopia at its secret core? Where this was once externalised from capitalist society, and located in other-worldly rewards, it has now come down from the heavens, and taken up its abode in the very materialities of capitalist production and consumption.

The conservatism of the people has been stolen by a social and economic system which can never deliver to them the security which is at the heart of their conservative impulse. It can never deliver these goods, because its inner dynamic requires the constant undermining of any peace and security that the people might create for themselves or seek to hold on to. Popular conservatism has placed its faith in the agent of its destruction.

Another form of conservatism expressed itself in the defensive structure of the traditional working-class culture which developed within nineteenth-century industrial communities. This culture equally sought to resist the intrusions of an industrial system into every aspect of people's lives. Later institutionalised within the Labour movement, it was first lived out at a practical level, as people endeavoured to mitigate for each other visitations of sickness, the death of children, the perishing of women in childbirth, a continuing inadequacy of basic resources. Much of this was the work of women, and was made possible through networks of kinship and neighbourhood, as well as the associations in the workplace, through trades unions, co-operative societies, burial clubs and friendly societies.

Significantly, this lived solidaristic practice was seen by Labour and socialist parties as holding in embryo the vision of a society that offered alternative values to those of capitalism. Yet again the closeness between popular conservatism and popular radicalism makes it difficult to distinguish one from the other. In this sense, even the most radical moment of transformation in Britain in the Forties carried within it a profoundly conservative resistance to the inflictions of capitalist society, as indeed, all true radicalism must. For true radicalism does not consist in tearing up a society by its roots (only industrialism does that), but on the contrary, returns to those roots in order to nourish their survival and sturdy growth.

The welfare state of the Forties represented another meeting between the energies of popular conservatism and popular radicalism. What could not have been realised at the time was that this strange encounter would finally give rise to a new conservatism, to which its radical counterpart still remains to be elaborated.

The welfare state seemed to offer what the people had always hoped for – security from cradle to grave. Was this a conservative hope or a radical ambition? What it actually produced was security for capitalism to set out on a period of expansion such as had not been seen since the exuberance of the early nineteenth century. This was the means whereby industrial capitalism was able to dissimulate its true nature behind the benign appearance of welfarism, and appeared to have realised the long promised, but constantly deferred, time of peace and plenty. Who could fail to be dissuaded from querulous opposition by such generous abundance as suddenly became available? Older ambiguities and antagonisms that persisted between the people's conservative hopes and capitalism's radical destructiveness seemed to have been dissolved. Clearly, the coming of the consumer society offered scope for a further and surely final transformation of conservatism, into a deep desire to maintain and keep what we have.

Conservatism had previously sought to safeguard what it valued most, to keep intact certain areas of experience against the invasion of industrial society, areas which were felt to be too intimate or too valuable to be thrown open to market penetration. The last half century appears to have shown us that the reservations and suspicions harboured by an earlier conservatism were groundless. In the post-war era, we believed we had reached the golden age, and it would go on for ever, changeless, assured and ultimately secure. The future promised more of the same, and the past was over and done with. No wonder nostalgia was banned. Whereas conservative ideologies had located the golden age in the past, and radical ideologies had placed it in the future, both were shown to be in error. The golden age was here and now, and it therefore ceased to make sense not live in the present.

Of course, just as there was a place for conservatism in this new epoch, so there was also room for a version of radicalism; only this radicalism was now confined to offering a permanent welcome to the novel changes that a benign capitalism would bring. For these had ceased to be a source of apprehension and injury to the people, but now seemed to be nothing more than a perpetual elaboration of what we had already seen and tasted and found to be good. In other words, revolutionary new products, fresh ways of satisfying old needs, radically improved commodities swept the market. All change and invention would henceforth take place under the benign superintendence of market forces. Infinite were the possibilities of the new; who could possibly ask for anything different? Conservatism became the conservation of a system which offered perpetual change. Uneasy alliances between radicalism and conservatism seemed to be over: their marriage had been consummated, and the society of consumption was their miraculous offspring.

But, alas, their mutability is perhaps the only shared long-term characteristic of human societies. Nothing remains still. Further changes are demanded by an industrial system which behind its smiling aspect, must go on industrialising or perish. But what was there left to industrialise? Strange new industries arose, almost behind our backs, and when we turned round we found ourselves confronted, no longer by a health service but by a health-care industry, by a music industry, a communications industry, an entertainment industry, an insurance industry. Markets were expected to be found everywhere, in education, in ideas, in hospitals. By the Eighties, the model of the business enterprise came to dominate every area of human experience. All institutions strove to approximate themselves to its style of human interaction. We all became customers, clients, consumers, punters, a humanity defined by its ability to purchase. Indeed, purchasing power came to be seen as the unique source of enablement in our lives. We were required to see our own lives as something to be managed and marketed. Any problems with image or self-presentation became the object of other people's labour. We were free to buy in any expertise we chose. And indeed, we found that we were compelled to buy in more and more of what we needed, to subcontract the resolution of our problems and difficulties. There were counsellors, advisers, consultants and therapists to whom we could turn, when we could no longer cope, manage, survive without the help of a multitude of agencies set up for that very purpose. How had all these been able to set up businesses in anticipation of our private woes and what we had thought were our individual needs? Who had told them that we would come knocking on their brass-plated doors, sitting abjectly in their muffled waiting rooms, anticipating the appointed hour on their threshold, nursing a pain that was becoming more unbearable by the minute?

How fortunate that we had so much more money to spend. And in spite of the access to wealth, how surprising that we felt no richer. Could it be that amid this extraordinary demonstration of riches, capitalism had found new ways of keeping us poor? Were new poverties, scarcely identifiable, the secret of a new phase of industrial expansion? How confusing to be told constantly that we were living through a period of de-industrialisation, and that we should be equipping ourselves to live in a post-industrial world! Was not the truth rather that industrialisation was continuing apace, but at levels which we had never dreamed it could penetrate, or which we might have felt were proof against its devastations?

And yet, it seemed, no one knew the causes of all the social evils which proliferated in this rich society. Crime rose, at times of recession and expansion alike. Easy explanations for this phenomenon froze on the lips of those who had asserted that crime was a product of poverty as well as those who had declared that crime was a consequence of the casino economy of the boom years. The experts said 'We do not know. It is too early to say. More research is required.' Similarly, as families increasingly broke down, fell apart, the very advocates of market penetration, those who had forbidden and ridiculed nostalgia, began to call for a return to family values, when it was clear that the forces of disruption which they themselves had set in train, were no respecters of institutions, no matter how cherished, or how essential to the well-being of society they might be.

When, after more than a hundred years of compulsory

education, levels of literacy were discovered to have fallen, the noisiest defenders of traditional educational methods were also to be found amongst those who derided everything that was not a commercial venture, and who created and celebrated all those marketed excitements and distractions and instantaneities that seduce young minds from the more rigorous paths required by serious study. Their only conception of what students might gain from exposure to education is that the young are so much raw material, to whom value may be added by educational processing. The industrial model is thus universalised. But then human beings have always been the rawest of industrial materials, to be shaped this way and that, to be manipulated and broken, smashed and re-assembled in the interests of whatever will make the greatest profit.

Nor are these more subtle social ills the only baleful consequence of this most recent phase of industrial reconstruction. Many older evils have also reappeared through the apparently altered surfaces of contemporary capitalism. Among the new and frightening shapes of exploitation, do we not greet the recurrence of poverty and unemployment almost with the relief at being in the presence of old friends? After all, if we are looking for continuities, connections with our own past, these have been our constant companions throughout the long journey down the years of industrial development. For a brief moment it appeared that they had been laid to rest, banished from the scenes of plenty of the affluent decades. Is it really their familiarity which makes their reappearance so unstartling? Why are we so undisturbed by the spread of poverty and unemployment? Perhaps it is because their presence in a society in which a majority of people remain extremely well-off is very different from a context in which most struggle at a level of bare sufficiency.

Where affluence is more generalised, there is more hope of avoiding the attentions of these spectres; there is more chance they will spare us. And after all, being poor and unemployed is not as bad as it used to be. We no longer let people starve in the streets; which is why those begging under bridges and sleeping in doorways are doing it because this is their choice.

If the homeless and those without livelihood no longer receive our sympathy, this is because we need all the sympathy we can get for ourselves; for, after all, we too have been deprived of so many things. We no longer have the generosity to hope for something better for them, because we have had social hope taken from us. What a grievous loss it is to have to acknowledge that no work with others for social change, no solidarities with a common purpose, no shared or collective activity can ever enhance or add to our lives again. The collapse of social hope throws us back on to the privatised possibilities of improvement. This means our lives can be extended only through the growth of our purchasing power. More money has to become the answer to everything, because all other answers have been cancelled.

We can now begin to perceive the suppressed connection between the great material improvements of the past forty years and the losses which came with them. This analysis has been vehemently denied by those who would see any attempt to make a balanced judgement of our experience of this period as an attack on the well-being of the people. 'You want to go back to poverty,' is the argument that silences all evaluation. Such tenderness for the condition of the people is not new. After all, the apologists of the slave trade were at pains to show how solicitous was the planter to preserve the life and health of his slaves, whereas free labour enjoyed no such protection. The brewers of Victorian England vigorously defended the right of the ordinary working man to his pint of refreshment, and in the streets they walked over the bodies of those corroded by alcohol. The advocates of child labour pointed out, not only that the system would totally collapse were it to be deprived of this amenity, but also that the employment of children provided useful and productive work for hands which, otherwise, the Devil would certainly employ in less honest toil.

In spite of all the attempts to prevent the connections being made, we can now more clearly see the link between the coming of capitalism's version of prosperity, and the half-articulated, obscurely felt losses that came with it. Such losses in this, the most spectacular phase of capitalism's gains, are substantial, as indeed they must be. They are experienced most fundamentally as a feeling of impotence, a depowerment, a disfranchisement – not in the electoral sense, of course, but where it really matters, in our control and influence over our own daily lives. How do people express their acknowledgement of the surrenders they have had to make in the trade-off between material gains and less palpable but just as significant losses? 'What can you do about it?'; 'You can't change the world'; 'Nothing I do will make any difference': these banal clichés contain depths of experience and disappointment which barely surface in the words themselves. They are the testimony of a profound sense of paralysis, immobilism and disengagement, all of which are inadmissible in a society which aims to have enabled, motivated and involved its people as never before. No wonder such complaints can only trail off inconclusively, as we make our peace with a system that has defeated us all. We do not have the strength to acknowledge the terms of the trade-off that has been taking place. These were never made clear amidst the sounds of noisy publicity and raucous advertising which promoted only the advantage of brand loyalty over commitment to deeper things; which promulgated all the free offers, the gifts and rewards, without even so much as hinting at the real price that would one day have to be paid for them.

The deeper surrenders, the forfeit of self-reliance and the relinquishing of hope that together we can change the world, these are the sub-political, even subliminal, experiences on which our current abject conservatism rests. This deformed conservatism is what makes us let pass that which we should challenge, accept what we know to be wrong, put up with things which we know are damaging ourselves and may be fatal to our children, permit to continue abuses which we should prevent. How can we make a stand against the youngsters tormenting the elderly, against the glue-sniffers destroying themselves under the stairs, against the cries of the woman being beaten next door, against the drug-sellers in the street-corner café, against the loneliness of the dirty old woman abandoned by her family, when it takes us all our time to find a place in which to stand ourselves to avoid being swept away by the tide? Why are we unable to act, to be effective in the neighbourhood where we live, in the local spaces which ought to be our undisputed home? We are afraid. We are afraid of getting involved, reprisals, people turning against us, incurring the anger of those stronger than we are, getting a brick through our window or shit through the door. Instead, all we can do is to scrimp and save, to work and hope that we will get the money to buy ourselves out of the wasteland in which we must live.

These are merely the exemplary sufferers from the cruder forms of our dispossession. In those areas where people pride themselves on having escaped these inflictions, they find they are prey to other terrors. On the private estates, the landscaped gardens, the Poggenpohl kitchens and Habitat drawing rooms provide only a more expensive decor for people's value-added suffering. Here, the fear of loss is always present; the loss of the man who returns to find the house empty and the woman on whom he had come to depend for so much has disappeared with a stranger; the employee of the transnational company who has been liberated so that he may seek something better, living in the dread of repossession, and the removal to who knows what squalid rooms; the anxiety of those returning home after a party, wondering if they will find the house in disorder, the familiar objects turned upside down, the jewellery gone, the valuables stolen; the fear of the woman robbed of what had seemed a rich and enduring social life by a sudden widowing, when she has never signed a cheque or paid a bill in her entire life; the parents wondering late at night just where their children are and with whom, while the police sirens wail in the distance. When these calamities happen, who are we to blame? There is no one there. We find we are alone; just as we were alone, and proud to be so, when we set out on these heroic labours of the improvement and bettering of our lives.

How lifeless and unsatisfying all our material well-being now seems. We now begin to realise why we had clung to them with such desperation: they gave us an impression of a security which we could decreasingly rely on elsewhere; they gave us the feeling that our lives were constantly expanding, when in ways that we did not then perceive they were shrinking and diminishing all the time. They came as substitutes for what was being taken away from us; we find now that they were no such thing; not substitutes at all, only symbols. If only we had been really materialistic and had been able to use and enjoy the material world for what it is, without investing it with miraculous properties to heal and to comfort, which only human beings can do. Alternatively, if only we really had been able to dispense with human comforts and could have taken true delight and genuine satisfaction in the material, and had regarded human attachments as mere frivolous addenda to the real business of living. At such terrifying moments we glimpse perhaps the paradox of our cowed and impotent conservatism; a conservatism which encases forms of unending disturbance and change. To sunder conservatism from conservation is a remarkable achievement; the more so, since that which it seeks to conserve is the very agent of global destruction. But this separation has one advantage. It illustrates more clearly the dilemmas before us, the nature of the choice that has to be made: the conserving of industrial society or the conservation of the planet.

Not for the first time, a true conservatism (preserving what is of value) is seen to be in opposition to its false namesake (maintaining industrial society); just as a true radicalism (fundamental change) stands against its counterfeit (endless uprootings by the industrial system). Such distinctions are not merely a question of semantics, a play on words: to call things by their proper names was always the first object of philosophy. This may help to explain the revulsion which the idea of any radical project inspires in the people of the West. So if change means changing a system that is already changing the way we live, and in such a way that it becomes ever less amenable to our control, no wonder people are terrified by the requirement of yet more change; one that would interfere with a dynamic of change, which has at least become familiar to us over the last 200 years. It is as though people were being told that we must not merely mount a running horse and change its direction, but do so while it is running headlong towards an abyss and rescue it in time. To call for change in such a context is like baying at the moon.

And yet we cannot help admiring those people who take a fishing smack to stand athwart the whaler; those who deliberately place themselves in the fall-out zone of atomic weapon experiments; those individuals who attend annual general meetings of major corporations in order to protest about bloody investments, only to be howled down by those who masquerade under the banner of a conservatism that would conserve nothing which threatened the health of their investments.

7

LEARNING FROM THE POOR

IN ORDER TO see what a truer conservatism might look like, we need to look at where it still exists among those people now being displaced from their habitats all over the Third World. Of course, they are often presented to us as dangerous revolutionaries and radicals, in the same way that those in Britain who resisted the exigencies of industrialism were presented. We may see no parallels or similarities between ourselves and those people who are resisting eviction from forests and fishing grounds, from ancestral lands and sacred places. It seems that their interests are directly contrary to ours, that they are our enemies. And indeed, they are our enemies, if we continue to cling to the changes demanded by our version of restless conservatism. For this demands that they be forcibly dispossessed of their livelihoods, their skills and resources, their careful custody of the treasures of nature, because we – or rather, our greedy industrial system – requires their forests, their minerals for our goods, it requires their labour to make things that will fill our shops and stores, and their land to grow our luxury produce.

If we look more carefully at the practice and tradition of tribal peoples worldwide, whether the Yanomami in Brazil, the Lumad of the Philippines, or the Adivasis of India, we would recognise that what they do is protect and maintain the resource base on which they depend. Industrial society has pillaged and ransacked and mined the resources of almost the whole world in order to create an economic growth which nevertheless has failed to achieve its alleged objective – the alleviation of human poverties. Quite the reverse, it has cunningly invented new ones, in order to sustain its self-expansion. The indigenous peoples have never left the earth poorer than they found it; or at least they never did until compelled to do so by colonial and industrial masters. Their supreme skill lay in their capacity for conservation, and this is why they pose such a threat to the false conservatives of the West. They want nothing more than to preserve and maintain what we have already heedlessly discarded, namely, the most precious resources on earth, both material and human.

What the tribal peoples make clear to us is that our industrial system depends upon a dual abuse of resources. What it squanders is a whole heritage of human abilities; the power of people to grow things for themselves, to make and do things for one another, to look after, comfort and nurture one another, to provide collectively for their own needs. These have all been degraded, undermined, ruined, in order to make way for substitutes for them; a vast proliferation of commodities and services, which, in turn, depend upon a second abuse of resources in the world – a using up of what industrial society has always been pleased to designate as raw materials, but what apparently less sophisticated, more 'primitive' peoples have held to be the very substance of the earth.

The creation of wealth involves a double impoverishment and a double wastage of vital resources. Nor do these two forms of impoverishing and wasting just casually co-exist. They are dynamically articulated one to the other. In many different ways, it is the depletion of both kinds of resources that the poor of the earth are seeking to resist. When they ask for a basic sufficiency and a fundamental security, they are claiming only a very modest share of the earth's resources, upon which their own resourcefulness and skills can then get to work.

If we were able to imagine a more creative interplay between human and planetary resources, we might have the makings of what has become a debased and meaningless ideal – a substainable human society. For the people of the West who have excavated and mined the known world have themselves also been excavated and mined in their turn; they have been emptied of their inner strengths and resiliences, their creative self-reliance, their power to imagine other ways of being in the world. No matter how much this process has impoverished other peoples in the world, it has conspicuously failed to enrich, in any but the most narrow sense, those who are supposed to be its beneficiaries. This is the truth behind the constant complaint of the rich that they are never rich enough.

Were we able to cease seeing the poor of the earth as our enemies, as rivals for scarce resources, as those who want what we've got, we might then perceive them for what they are – the embodiment of our best hopes. They can offer us both instruction and wisdom, if we will recognise them. This is no easy task, given the dehumanising imagery in which their life-situation is shown to us. For even the most sensitive TV documentaries are rarely little more than peepshows. At best they offer us insight into an archaic way of life, which, charitably, we may wish to defend for them against loggers and timber companies and mineral prospectors, but in which we discern little of relevance to our own advanced way of life.

Yet our lives are interconnected in so many ways; and they provide us with a mirror image of our own situation. One basic thing we might learn is that even their abundant human resources are over-stretched by material poverty; while our human resources are under-utilised through commodity substitution. Further, we might understand that we are oppressed by our excessive dependency upon material resources, while they are deeply damaged by basic insufficiencies of the materialities of food, health and shelter. Those who speak glibly of 'an interdependent world' fail to mention how an 'interdependence' based upon profound inequalities is no such thing, but is actually an apology for dominance. A true interdependence would involve a real sharing, in which we stop depriving them of the basic necessities which they lack, and could provision ourselves from the rich store of human creativity which they deploy.

There are other lessons to be learnt. Enough people from the West have found things of value in the cultures of the

Third World, not only of 'unspoiled' indigenous peoples, but also of farming communities, and even urban slum-dwellers, for us to gain a sense of the qualities of a different way of life. We who live at the centre of an imperial and universalising culture find it difficult to take such testimonies seriously. It is always tempting to dismiss those who report back to us as romantics, escapists, even misfits, yet there is a common patterning in these experiences.

An anthropology student says:

> On an anthropological expedition in my second year at university, I came into contact with a tribe in the Peruvian Amazon. There are about 20,000 people in the whole tribe, who hunted, fished and grew things. In the world's terms, they were very poor – everything they had they had made from the forest. But they seemed happy. They lived in harmony with the forest, and their lives in their small communities seemed balanced, too.
>
> Most anthropologists who go to remote areas come back with the same story. Being with the people becomes more important for them than doing anthropology. When I came back I was less of an anthropologist, and I was suffering from culture shock.
>
> I remember at one time I had to move out from the jungle village and go to the town. Suddenly, I was bombarded with demands for money. It was a terrible shock, when for three months you haven't put your hand in your pocket, whilst living with what are supposed to be some of the poorest people on earth.
>
> There is nowhere on earth I have ever felt so secure. The village was womb-like. I had such a strong feeling of security. Going into a really different, a quite alien culture, I felt helpless. I couldn't do all the things they could do really well. I even fell over walking in the forest. They were very patient teachers.
>
> And they laughed differently to us. Not nervous laughter, but with their whole body, like a wave.[11]

In her book, *Ancient Futures*, Helena Norberg-Hodge describes how she visited Ladakh for the first time in the mid-Seventies. She was so overwhelmed by the beauty of the landscape and of the culture, that she remained, and has devoted herself to the preservation and enhancement of the traditional Ladakhi way of life.

Ladakh is a small Buddhist enclave in Jammu and Kashmir in the Himalayan rainshadow. It is 11,500 feet above sea level, and the traditional culture is based upon raising sheep and goats, yaks and cows, and the cultivation of barley and wheat. It has a population of 130,000.

In Ladakh, I felt completely safe; as a woman I had always been aware that I was a potential victim of violence. One evening, I saw a group of men coming towards me from the opposite direction. It was dusk, and I realised that here, I didn't have to be frightened. Until then, I had accepted the idea there would always be conflict, because human beings are aggressive by nature. I had been convinced that culture didn't play a significant part in shaping human beings. But in Ladakh, I found that peace was a way of life. Peace, co-operation and mutual aid formed the basis of survival, and it really worked. That had all sorts of implications. I saw my own industrial culture in a different light. My context for judging human beings shifted dramatically.

Until then, the only differences I'd seen had all been within industrial culture – Sweden, America, Germany, Austria, France, England. I had been in Mexico, and I was moved by the Indians there, their way of being. But in retrospect I realised that their culture had been starved and made introverted by centuries of Western occupation. The openness and joy were gone from the Indians in America; but the Himalayas had protected people by their remoteness. I saw the West relativised.

I think I had been quite well adjusted in my own culture, but the lack of roots – I moved around so much – gave me an openness to other influences. I'd always felt vaguely that I'd been born at the wrong time, but I assumed that was just a romantic longing for an earlier age. I didn't see there was an alternative; and I believed in progress.

I am convinced that the Ladakhis are much happier than we are. I find less resistance from women to that feeling. Margaret Mead, who had lived in Samoa, said essentially the same thing. Her experience was that the culture was more peaceable and co-operative, individuals more balanced psychologically. After she died, a male anthropologist came out attacking her, destroying her and her arguments, saying she was just a young impressionable female, influenced by her professor in America, and that she'd come with preconceived notions, and hadn't really lived with the people, or even spoken the language. They can't say that about me, so they say I'm mad.[12]

What was it in Margaret Mead's work that had so disturbed her colleagues that it had to be invalidated? Was it because she had suggested that the children of Samoa were in some important ways less ignorant than the highly educated children of the West?

None of the facts of sex or of birth are regarded as unfit for children, no child has to conceal its knowledge for fear of punishment or ponder painfully over little-understood occurrences. Secrecy, ignorance, guilty knowledge, faulty speculations resulting in grotesque conceptions which have far-reaching results, a knowledge of the bare physical facts of sex without a knowledge of the accompanying excitement, of the fact of birth without the pains of labour, of the fact of death without the fact of corruption – all the chief flaws in our fatal philosophy of sparing children a knowledge of the dreadful truth – are absent in Samoa. Furthermore, the Samoan child who participates intimately in the lives of a host of relatives has many and varied experiences upon which to base its emotional attitudes. Our children, confined within one family circle (and such confinement is becoming more and more frequent with the growth of cities and the substitution of apartment houses with a transitory population for a neighbourhood of householders), often owe their only experience of birth or death to the birth of a younger brother or sister or the death of a parent or grandparent . . . the youngest child in a family where there are no deaths may grow to adult life without ever having had any close knowledge of pregnancy, experience with young children, or contact with death.[13]

If there are often traces of defensiveness in accounts of other cultures, it is because such testimonies are consistently ridiculed as romanticised reports of a way of life which those who extol them have merely visited. If they knew the culture better, they would realise that the virtuous primitives whose praises they sing share an identical human nature with us; and are capable of as much cruelty, greed and deception as could ever be found at home. If they appear to live in collective peace, in harmony with nature, this is because their horizons have remained so limited, their vision constrained by poverty, their desires unawakened by what they have never seen, and therefore never learned to want. As soon as they come into contact with the superior possibilities of industrial society, they will stop at nothing to lay hands upon the good things they have seen. If they seem happy, is this not rather the numb acceptance of their inability to change anything in their lives? They are stuck in a time warp, and it is their destiny, as well as their deepest desire, to join the modern world.

Of course, it will be conceded, there is a calm and a peace and a certain picturesqueness in these archaic survivals. There is something nice about these societies, but whether we like it or not, their days are numbered. There is no room for sentimentality; it is the right of such people to belong to the global community, to have access to all the benefits which the West possesses, and which permit its travellers to pay extended visits to these remote corners of the earth. Those who argue for the preservation of virtually extinct ways of life are setting themselves up as human zookeepers, stunting people in their development, as though they existed for our entertainment. The time has come for them to participate fully in development processes that cannot be stopped. Wild romantics who want to turn back the clock, or even more impossible, to keep it fixed at a particular time, must be reminded that these people, when given the opportunity, will in any case vote with their feet, and make their way to the nearest city.

These voices, which dominate all discussion in the West, are the bearers of a very old story. They tell how the West has always been the foundation and origin of civilisation, and of its mission to spread out slowly from the enlightened core to the furthest corners of the globe, and to bring all people, no matter how benighted, into its liberating embrace. Its universalising pretensions have never altered, although they have taken different forms. If the threatened ways of life of tribal and indigenous peoples, relatively small enclaves that remain outside the reach of the imperial power, are so disturbing to us, this is because they demonstrate, however sketchily, that there are alternative ways of living in the world, even alternative ways of structuring our societies, answering our needs, regulating our economies. They are essentially the heretics, whose conversion to our superior ways is both necessary and inevitable. The tones in which these romantic accounts are dismissed are mild and measured; in fact, the voices are those of intolerance, of zealotry and rigid orthodoxy. It is not so much that these societies do not want to survive, nor even that they could not survive, but that they must not be allowed to survive, because they contain a vestigial but continuing criticism of the way we are.

These testimonies are upsetting, not simply because they might be true, because these societies might actually possess the qualities which such romantics discover, but because their accounts imply absences they perceive in the societies from which they come. The West prides itself that its society offers everything. That there might be glaring gaps and deficiencies in its spectacular provision it will not contemplate. If people return from primitive societies with stories of the value of participating, of sharing the preparation of food, fishing, taking care of children, celebrating their survival, what does this say of our prized individualism which denies that people can do anything together but compete? When they tell us that tribal people seem open and friendly, what does this tell us about the defensiveness towards each other which we have had to learn, the mistrust which has become second nature? When we hear of people being less differentiated, of the boundaries of personality being more fluid, of the ability to merge in collective rites and ceremonies, how shall we then interpret our own loneliness, our own inability to make contact with others? When they speak of the achievement of exalted states of mind, forms of changed consciousness brought about by the recounting of legend and myth, the singing and dancing of their lives, how are we then to understand a dependency on chemicals in order to make life bearable for so many of our people, let alone our mimicking of rituals of transcendence through crack or ecstasy?

So of course we must deny that these people possess anything that we might lack or want. Of course we must insist that those who say otherwise are at best deceived romantics, at worst disturbed crackpots. In this way we are excused even from having to consider how we might go about the process of learning, let alone tackle the difficulties that would certainly be involved.

Nor should we imagine that it is only these pre-industrial societies that can offer unsettling insights into the way we live, although these are peculiarly poignant since they are on the point of being extinguished by the long reach of industrialism. We have already seen how the inhabitants of the slums of the Third World cities can rekindle for us suppressed memories of our own past. They can also show us where we might seek the resources to resist the further ravages of industrialisation to which we are constantly subjected. Out of the most squalid and repelling circumstances in which it is possible for human beings to survive also come examples of the ingenuity, creativity and skill by which people seek to make good the gross deficit of material things in their lives. Of the pavement-dwellers in Bombay a woman worker says of the building of huts:

> Women know how to use space – nine feet by five – with great efficiency. Ask them, 'Where do you keep your clothes? Where do you keep the water vessel? Where do you wash?' They are skilled architectural designers. These are the strengths that get lost when people are decanted into bricks-and-mortar flats designed by men. For instance, women will know exactly where to build benches above the level to which the water floods in the monsoon. They will know what kinds of material are more suitable for marshy or stony ground. Women build their own stoves for cooking, some of them miracles of invention. They don't waste space with physical partitions, but demarcate areas with goods, a bed, some utensils. They'll paint the wall against which the hut is leaning

white; they'll leave an aperture for the smoke to escape, a space to catch the cool breezes.[14]

What we might learn from pre-industrial peoples is that with sufficient material resources allied to creative human energies, a high quality of life may be attained. What we might learn from the slum-dwellers is that no matter how lacking the material resources are, human beings are capable of prodigious achievements in making a half-decent life, while still falling short of what they need. What we might learn from the advanced industrial societies is that the excessive reliance on material resources leads to a suppression of human creativity, and that such an imbalance means that a decent life still remains elusive. If we were to discover that such an imbalance was the basis on which our social and economic system is constructed, and that its continued well-being depends upon the worsening of this imbalance, what could we possibly do to correct it?

If we have been taught to look down upon the peoples of the Third World, this is perhaps understandable, given the way in which we have also been encouraged to condescend to our own ancestors, even to our own past selves. Just as racism is the bequest of imperialism, so the cancelling of memory is the inheritance of industrial 'progress'. No wonder industrial society wants nothing to do with what it is swift to stigmatise as romanticism or nostalgia.

There is so much we need to retrieve from the shadows of our ignorance and our forgetting. We forget that the opposite of poverty is not wealth, but sufficiency. We were poor for so long that we could not escape the knowledge that more resources were absolutely essential for our well-being. It was a short step, but a ruinously fateful one, when we slipped into the belief that the growth of freedom was synonymous with the growth of wealth. Because it was obvious that it was a lack of money that brought misery into our lives, it began to seem plausible, not only that more money would rescue us, but that yet more money would guarantee a growing happiness. While it is impossible to say exactly what level of goods and services are necessary for a truly human life, we can say with some certainty that we have now gone far beyond any reasonable definition of sufficiency. And the fact that even the idea of sufficiency now seems irretrievable is an indication of how far our very lives have become functions of an economic system whose constant expansion is by no means there to serve human beings.

Part of the work of recovering and remembering needs to be carried out within the mainstream political ideologies of our culture. When we look at the mutations of contemporary conservatism, it is difficult to recall that we, too, have had our tradition of conserving and keeping, of thrift and husbandry. Those who doubt that what is currently called conservatism is a sham and counterfeit, have only to consider how frugality and self-denial not so long ago were the supreme conservative virtues. Were not deferred pleasures supposed to have been all the sweeter for being postponed, and capable thereby of being doubly savoured, for they could also be enjoyed in anticipation? How can we reconcile this with a conservatism that urges us on to instant enjoyments and ever-accelerating consumption? When economists lament that consumer confidence has failed to return to the High Streets and that the economy is therefore still in recession, we wonder whether we should feel guilty that we are not spending our money at a sufficient speed to restore the economic fortunes of our country. To consume is to be patriotic. We wonder if the already vast debts are not enough, and whether it is our duty to incur even more for the public good. Yet we hear a strangely conservative voice at the back of our minds. It seems to be saying: 'What I can't pay for I go without'; 'Neither a borrower nor a lender be'; 'Everything you see here is paid for'. Sometimes this original conservatism is echoed in public rhetoric, but it is evidently something not to be taken seriously, a bit like the vicar's Sunday sermon; uplifting, but scarcely practical in the real world. It doesn't seem so long since we heard much about 'good housekeeping' and 'cutting our coat according to our cloth', 'living within our means'. That all this was happening in the decade when debts multiplied is calculated to obscure further the true nature of conservatism.

Saving up, keeping, maintaining, putting by, preserving, taking care of resources and passing them on; leaving a better inheritance to the children. Of course, today's conservatives also boast of creating 'a generation of inheritors'. They speak in rapturous terms of 'money cascading down the generations'. (The fruit-machine imagery is singularly apt.) What they don't say is that the generation of inheritors will inherit another legacy, and one certainly brought about by the creation of the wealth they will possess. This bequest will be one of irreversible poisonings, barren fields, pollutions, resource wars, climatic disaster, which none of their wealth will buy them exemption from. No matter how much money the children may inherit, much good will it do them if money proves unable to restore what the making of money has certainly destroyed.

In parallel there has always been a popular tradition of taking pride in people's ability to stretch and amplify limited resources, to make a little go a long way, to make ends meet, to make do and mend, to make a meal out of a few odds and ends, to improvise, to eke out, to share the little they had when someone dropped in at mealtimes. Nothing is ever wasted in this house, they used to boast: no crusts, no parings, no cheese rind that couldn't be used in one way or another. If a child threw bread on the fire, she was told that she was feeding the devil. Hands were never still: they knitted and sewed and repaired shoes, they made clothes and chairs and tables, they tended allotments and fed chickens. How remote this now seems, how antiquated by the fall-apart luxury, the throwaway opulence of all that has displaced it. These traditions evolved because people never had enough. This did not mean they were unworthy or ignoble; nor did it mean they should have been cast away when more adequate resources became available. To work with this ingenuity of need was the objective of labour movements; nevertheless, these became involuntary agents of its destruction. For if this conserving sensibility had been allied to the improved material circumstances, it could have saved millions of truly needy people elsewhere from death by hunger and sickness. But although labour and socialist movements imagined that

they could build a new society upon this popular resourcefulness, it was capitalism that determined the structures of the
post-war edifice, in which that resourcefulness had to be
scattered and squandered.

These popular traditions of frugality were not ideologies,
they were living practices. They were the way ordinary
women and men carried out their daily lives and taught
their children to follow them. That all this should have been
discarded overnight was a grievous loss, and grievously we
are paying for it. To want to re-evaluate and revalue these
traditions has nothing to do with a desire to *return*, to inflict
a life of penny-pinching misery and privation upon the
people. It is rather to wish to restore a sense of balance
against the celebration of waste, the sanctification of the
superfluous. That we have developed a capacity to see this
as normal, even as essential, is an indication of immeasurable
losses; loss of judgement and discrimination among them.

8

THE CONDITION OF THE RICH

THERE IS LITTLE incentive for the people of the Western world to make the necessary acts of retrieval, to go through the labour of remembering. They are safe at home, the long journey over. Their refuge is the commodious construct of consumerism. This edifice is to its recent and grateful occupants what the mansions of the blest must have appeared to the starved imagination of their industrial forebears. It seems a definitive asylum, a haven from the insecurities and exclusions of a culture of poverty.

A strong sense that struggle has ceased pervades the West. The people have reached their destination, even fulfilled their destiny. Those who had predicted that the people were bound to remain forever estranged from capitalism have been conclusively shown to have been in error. Almost overnight, it seemed, the world had changed. All that was required was that people should accept with due gratefulness the better times that were upon them. All that remained for them to do was to cut out the coupons and get the free gifts. Never was epochal change achieved with such effortless amiability.

People experienced this as freedom, and, in a way, it was. All the careful husbandry, the thrift and frugality, the self-denial and inventiveness were suddenly shown up in a new light. Suddenly they ceased to be virtues. These human qualities were metamorphosed into their opposites: penny-pinching meanness, stinginess, a waste of time and energy. How cramped and grudging these lives were discovered to have been. In their place a new set of virtues – an expansive, generous, no-expense-spared sensibility – emerged. When we glanced back, we wondered, not so much why things had changed so swiftly, but rather how we could ever have lived like that. We were now liberated from the tyranny of the cheapest cut, the most inexpensive goods, shop-soiled materials, inferior produce. We were as good as our masters, or at least, our money was as good as theirs, and appeared to purchase the same high-quality goods, the same desirable styles of living. Oh happy moment.

All we could now want was that it should last for ever. It became our most cherished axiom that there could be no going back. Progress had become a mechanical stairway that led to a higher plane of consumption on the next floor of the universal supermarket. All we had to do was to stand still, in order to be wafted upwards, effortlessly, endlessly. It was a materialised version of the Sunday school story of Jacob's ladder, where Jacob meets the angel and encounters the divine. If we had listened more carefully, we might have remembered the rest of the story – how Jacob was forced to wrestle with the angel in order to gain a true blessing, and how the result of the fight was a wounded hip, which he carried with him for ever.

Almost before we knew it, we had joined the rich; or at least, we had entered into our apprenticeship in the ways of the wealthy of the world. What we now had, and wished to hang on to, gave us a stake in the system. Without noticing, we became curiously estranged from the poor, which meant, not only the people of the Third World, but also the selves we had been. We could measure the distance that now separated us from them through our fluency in a language of condemnation which we were well versed in, because we had for so long heard it applied to us. We, too, had once been described, within our own hearing, as feckless, lazy, improvident. If the poor cast envious eyes upon us, we knew what we had to say: 'All you have to do is work hard like us, then you'll have what we've earned.'

Yet what had we done to earn these rewards? Nobody said. The truth is we had had the supreme sagacity to be born at the right time in the right place. People who have been blessed by good fortune rarely see the favours they have received as gratuitous. It is never hard to find reasons for deserving them, and merit is rarely difficult to discern somewhere, in even the most unworthy individual, if he has money in his pockets.

It comes as no surprise that people have no urgent wish to change such a fortunate order. However, if the mansions of consumerism really were the dwelling places of satisfied needs and longings fulfilled, of sorrows assuaged, and yearnings stilled; if they really were the home of dreams realised, of antique human visions made manifest, surely there would be in these places of abundance less strife, less violence, less anger, less frustration, less cruelty. Even the heart's desire, that most elusive of human needs, ought to have been found there.

That this has not occurred is apparent to everyone. These societies which ought to have more than enough to satisfy human needs, are nevertheless inhabited by needy people: people preying upon each other, abusing one another, ripping one another off, in the aptly violent popular image, not trusting anyone. People are constantly finding each other out 'as they really are', showing themselves in their true colours, taking each other for all they can get. In other words, they are perpetually revealing that version of their nature that provides such fuel for the motors of consumption, a nature which is mistakenly declared to be quintessentially human. If we behave in this way, is it not because, far from being free to express what we truly are, we are compelled to express the dynamic of the system which we inhabit and which inhabits us?

Of course, it will be argued, the turbulence, the frantic quality of our happy-ever-after, comes from the discovery of new human needs and wants, novel desires, which remained formerly obscured because of the more urgent priorities to which we had to attend. If you don't know where the next meal is coming from, it is not a social disgrace if the souffle doesn't rise properly. Now that basic needs have been met, the argument continues, we can set about the fulfilment of more sophisticated and arcane requirements.

The violence that disfigures our society is explained away

as merely the inevitable consequence of the enlarged freedoms, the increased mobility, the escape from narrowing constraints, that people now enjoy; this is a more subtle version of a nineteenth-century explanation that its social evils were only the unfortunate 'price of progress'; by-products, details in the crucial business of wealth-creation.

Yet it remains open to question whether even our most basic human needs have indeed been met. We might ask what happened to the need for security, for conviviality, for fellowship, for constancy, for mutuality, for social hope? For these remain aching absences in our treasured showhouse. Not only do these needs remain unanswered, but many of them are actively and consistently subverted by a system to which the answering of need is always subordinate to the creation of needs. If needs were truly answered, people would no longer feel compelled to buy the simulations and counterfeits and makeshifts and substitutes that they must be persuaded to buy.

Nothing could be more menacing to the well-being of capitalism than that its people should avow themselves content with what they have, and satisfied with what they can give to each other. This is the secret nightmare of capitalism, and in order to forestall such a calamity, it sets in motion an elaborate machinery of denial. Its operations ensure that contentment is never available and satisfaction never to be had wherever its writ runs. In such a context, even when we seek to answer simple needs, we find that we have also set up a more complicated way of frustrating them. In this way, how often, when we wish to express our affection and tenderness for our children, do we go and buy some material token, some fashionable instant emblem of good parenting, rather than sweeping them up in our arms and giving them something of ourselves? All our liberation and all our independence culminate in the ability to go shopping.

Even from the earliest period of industrialism, there emerged what has become a tradition of criticism of industrial society. This argues that such a society is bound to be dehumanising, both through its forms of labour and in its modes of consumption. This critique has by no means been invalidated as time has gone by. But in recent years, there has emerged a new, and even more damaging moral and material indictment of industrialism. It was always plain that the manufacturing districts if Victorian England were injurious to health and life, produced pollutants and poisons that damaged those who worked there. But it was always possible for a privileged minority to buy themselves out of the squalors of Engel's Manchester or Mayhew's London, to avoid the more noxious by-products of industrial life. The rich could always live away from the prevailing wind, on the Western heights of the city, in their imaginative Gothic architecture, surrounded by kitchen gardens, arbours and conservatories, with sturdy evergreens to shield them from such traffic as passed their secluded doors. For them it was possible, even essential, to avoid the foul exhalations of the canal, the stench of the rag-and-bone shop, the effluvia of the factory. Even to see these things became an affront to their refinement and good taste. The poor, on the other hand, were kept to their own quarters, and nobody, surely, needed to have business there. So repellent were the dwellings of the poor, that to leave them became an obsession. It became the object of anyone who could save enough money, to buy a passage from these sites of desolation.

And it worked. The Victorian suburb is perhaps the most moving monument to the almost superhuman exertions of people desperate for their families to escape, to better themselves, to purchase some degree of protection against the contaminants and pollutants. Once this had been accomplished, it was possible to ensure that the children would grow up in the sweet clear air, that the water they drank would be clean, that the soil in which the fresh vegetables grew would remain free of poisons. There were no two ways about it: in this sense, money could buy what was worthwhile, it could purchase privilege.

It is a genuine and poignant irony, that at the very moment when these privileges seem to have been made available to a majority of the people in the West, money should begin to lose its power to buy its owners the immunity it once vouchsafed them. That money, the great enabler, the opener of all

83

doors, the motivator of all actions, the speaker of all languages, might begin to lose its lustre, to dwindle and to lose its potency, to shed its mysterious dynamism, and might return to its sometime inert and lifeless condition, strikes terror into the heart of the system. That money might lose its value through inflation we have become accustomed to; but that money might die through its inability to purchase what we most urgently need for our survival is scarcely to be contemplated.

Yet this is what is happening. For the extension of industrialism throughout the world has involved such an intensification of industrial processes, that the damage caused pervades even the remotest enclaves of privilege that the earth can offer. Of course, in the early period, the rich were buying themselves double protection – not only from the pollution of industrialism, but also protection from the attention of those disadvantaged by their wealth, what were variously described as the mob, the rabble, the hands. And this latter shield is still available today. The rich quarters of the Third World city still seem like another world: in Manila, as you pass into the prosperous districts, you go through a frontier, as though entering another country. There is a checkpoint, a yellow-and-black pole, a bullet-proof glass booth. In Rio, the rich live in steel cages with spiked railings that curve outwards, behind triple locks. But the security this purchases is becoming increasingly illusory. The most obvious characteristic of global pollution is that it does not discriminate. It may be possible to avoid the chemical smog and city fumes, and to drink bottled water; but, who can escape the carcinogens and toxins in the food chain; whose private gene-pool can gain immunity from the effects of radiation; who has yet constructed a private ozone layer to ward off skin cancer; where is the privileged micro-climate that will resist global warming; who is going to replicate the biodiversity of the global commons in his private estate?

The potency of this argument for a different kind of change, and for another form of conservatism, derives from its inclusiveness. It is a form of radicalism from which the most privileged will also benefit. But it has to be realised that those who declared that Western affluence was an irreversible process, that there could be no going back, were fundamentally mistaken. The security offered by a vast access of wealth rested on the shakiest of foundations. If the people were in error in their assumption that the new epoch could last forever, the possessing classes were also mistaken in their calculation that the growth in income made possible by increased industrial production would attach the people for ever to a system without end. The effects of this double miscalculation are what we must face.

We can now see that all the negative consequences of the system's success have been discounted. Not only have the destructive effects upon human beings – both rich and poor – been suppressed, but so equally have the malign results upon the resource base of the earth. For orthodox economics, all these phenomena have been merely 'externalities', that is to say, simply not counted in the balance sheet of profit and loss. But these neglected externalities do not go away because we choose not to count them. They now threaten to invade and overwhelm the lives of us all. We have become so habituated to the industrial system's version of change and disruption, that we have come to regard these as natural. We have always adapted ourselves, however painfully, to each and every change, and then got on with our lives as best we could to await the next one. What we find it difficult to imagine is that the next set of changes might be of a kind and magnitude as to escape even the ubiquitous control of the global industrial system.

The truth is that if we wish to avoid even deeper levels of disruption and suffering than anything we have hitherto experienced, we shall have to develop quite different ways of responding. It is no longer good enough to see the world as a place where things just happen to us, take us unawares, arrive out of the blue. For how we act, or even more significantly, fail to act, in the world also has its consequences.

The concept of consciousness has always haunted radical political activity. It would be a strange irony if, at the moment when that radical enterprise in which class consciousness was to have played such a crucial role is being consigned to the rubbish dump of history, consciousness itself were to be a casualty of a more general discrediting. For we in the West seem to have slipped into a form of unconsciousness, an unknowing, which is at odds with the urgency of the times. We know and do not know. We know that there is something deeply wrong in the way we are living; but also know that any serious modification in that way would inevitably undermine democracy, freedom, individual choice, and all the other sacred attributes which uniquely distinguish our advanced civilisation. What we do not know is the vital and dynamic link between what we feel to be wrong and what cannot be changed.

As we go about managing our daily lives, choosing between the 12,000 items available on our supermarket shelves, do we sense that this partial freedom is gained at the expense of a real loss of diversity in the world, the extinction of thousands of plant and animal forms? As we select Brazilian mangoes or pineapples from the Ivory Coast for our dessert, does something stir in our memory about people dying for want of the nutrition which they once grew for themselves on the land which now furnishes us with these agreeable fruits?

Yes, but. Haven't we heard all this before? Isn't this wearily familiar? To be honest, isn't it yet another attempt to make us feel guilty? We all know what's wrong, but we're tired of having our noses rubbed in it. We have learnt to live with our guilt.

To know what is wrong and to believe that nothing can be done about it is perhaps a working definition of the kind of freedom we enjoy in this society. It is to be immobilised, captive, enslaved. It is not that we acquiesce voluntarily in injustice and deprivation in the world, but that we are compelled to. The unspoken implication is that if we were to think seriously of interfering with the social and economic relationships of the world, it is we who would come off worse. We would have to forfeit privileges which we suspect are probably won at the expense of others, although we don't know them personally. Our reluctant consent is gained by means of blackmail. If you want to keep what you've got, if you don't want anyone close to you to get hurt, keep your mouth shut. Of course, there are no blackmail notes, no pieces of ear arrive through the post, no secret mail-drop for the ransom. Nevertheless, this relationship permeates everything we do, all that we own, every possession we have, every amenity we enjoy.

We should feel guilty in order that we might be free. It is the repudiation of being made to feel guilty, the twilit half-recognition of the link between our privilege and their penalty that give rise to the tension, the feeling of being trapped, the anguish of being unable to move. The denial that we are guilty prevents us from being able to acknowledge our unfreedom. So, we keep our heads down, we get on with the business of living, we put our expiatory energy into earning so that we may attain a sense of that precarious freedom, which remains elusive in spite of the official rhetoric about our democratic freedoms and our hard-won liberties. Liberty is indeed hard to win, and we have yet to win it.

But the guilt we need to take upon ourselves is not an individual, privatised guilt, to be picked over endlessly and inconclusively in the secrecy of our own heart. Our involvement in a global system of exploitation is not a private matter: it is shared and collective. And the only way in which it can be dealt with is collectively. But here is another aspect of the process that keeps us in our place. All collective work has been disgraced, denigrated, rendered inconceivable when everything that is significant occurs in private.

For if we acknowledge this guilt, we shall not continue to deny the connections that exist between the parody of the fearful good life which we lead, with all its violence and insecurity, and the reality of the bad life, with all its violence and insecurity that the majority of humankind must endure. The rewards for such recognition might look dubious, compared with the substantial compensations for keeping silent even within ourselves. But the real reward would lie in breaking the spell that has laid us under an enchantment that has turned us to stone, petrified us indeed. We would stretch our limbs and move, return to life; a renewal of vigour and energy would restore our connectedness with each other and our ability to act and to effect *our* changes in the world. We will rediscover the powers and abilities that have lain unused within us, superfluous in a world of sterile abundance that impoverishes and undermines and, in the end, does not satisfy. The questions that have tugged at us through the long numbness of our immobilism – 'But what can you do about it?' 'What difference will it make?' 'Who's going to listen to me?' – will be answered.

No one has ever claimed that it is easy to be part of a movement of liberation. The argument for accepting the way things are is always overwhelming. No abuses have ever been so damaging that they could not find apologists falling over themselves to explain why these were essential to the well-being of the world. No injustices were ever so unbearable that the powerful could not advance conclusive arguments as to their ennobling and beneficial effects upon their victims.

Eric Williams, in *Capitalism and Slavery*, gives an account of the arguments used against the abolitionists, on the grounds that they themselves were necessarily implicated in the global slave system:

> The abolitionists were boycotting the slave-grown produce of the British West Indies, dyed with the Negro's blood. But the very existence of British capitalism depended upon the slave-grown cotton of the United States, equally connected with slavery, and polluted with blood. The West Indian could legitimately ask whether 'Slavery was only reprehensible in countries to which their members do not trade, and where their connections do not reside.' The answers given were curious. The person who received slave-grown produce from America dealt in the produce of labour performed by slaves who were not his fellow-subjects, and there was not, in the slavery of the United States, any evidence of that destruction of human life which was one of the most appalling features of the system in the British West Indies. The boycotters of West Indian sugar sat upon chairs of Cuban mahogany, before desks of Brazilian rosewood, and used inkstands of slave-cut ebony; but 'it would do no good to go round and inquire into the pedigree of every chair and table'. In a country like England total abstinence from slave produce was impossible, unless they wished to betake themselves to the woods and live on roots

and berries. As the Newcastle abolitionists argued, only 'the unnecessary purchase of one iota of slave produce involves the purchaser in the guilt of the slaveholder'.[15]

The invitation to the dissident to take a personal exit from industrial society is always the argument of last resort to those who are resolved to protect its continuing development at all costs. When people are accused of being hypocritical because they will boycott the produce of one tyrannical regime, only to accept quite happily the commodites of another equally corrupt or unjust, they are being taunted with their individual impotence. But it is actually the unthinkability of collective action that makes such taunts possible. Any suggestion that the development of industrial society might be amenable to human control always brings forth an incredulous scorn: 'You want to take us back to the stone age,' they will say when confronted with the most modest attempt to restrict the destruction caused by the excesses of the motorcar. You can't pick and choose which aspects of progress you will accept. You must take the rough with the smooth. It is clear that industrial society offers 'a package', a totality, which is non-negotiable; the entirety in which it must be accepted is a caricature of holism. Everything it produces is essentialised. Our freedoms finally consist in a clear-sighted recognition of the indivisibility of the goods from the evils within industrial society. It is clear from the cowed and subservient response to our creation that society has become the equivalent of a natural phenomenon, or rather a force of nature, because that suggests something organic and irresistible. If our freedom means acknowledging the inevitable, then our freedom is to recognise our unfreedom, and to accept whatever maimings and woundings may be necessary to live within its constricting boundaries and limitations. No wonder the first stirrings of a different consciousness are so disturbing. To feel a desire to take control over the shaping of our own world is to experience an obscure sense of sin, of impiety, as though we were questioning the sacred.

The prohibition on the use of our own powers and capacities

to change the way things are is supported by a vast apparatus of superior expertise and knowledge. Indeed, whole industries exist whose function, ostensibly to enlighten us, is actually to reinforce our own impotence and ignorance. In fact, much of the work of the advanced societies is concerned with keeping vital connections hidden. This is reflected in a complex division of labour, in which our purposes are invisible to one another. This reassures us that while we do not know what is going on, there are others who do; that what appears to be out of control is safe in the capable hands of experts, scientists, professional, pundits, consultants, savants of all kinds. This has another advantage, too – it absolves us from any responsibility for the wrongs of the world, as well as for findings solutions to them. 'They'll come up with something'; 'They'll find a way round it.'; 'They'll find the answer'; 'They'll invent something'. After all, they always have done. People have been prophesying doom ever since the beginnings of industrialism.

People resisted the building of the railways, because they said the iron monsters would scar the countryside for ever. And now, some of the most picturesque sites and conservation areas in Britain run along disused railway lines. It was said that the great urban centres would always remain concentrations of disease and sickness; yet they cured TB, smallpox, cholera, diphtheria. It was said that to live in the industrial conurbations was an unnatural way of life, which would lead people into vice, and would result in the breakdown of all natural bonds and ties of affection; instead, people found they were free to determine their own relationships, to escape from the constraints of custom and tradition in choosing those they would associate with. It was even suggested that industrialism would so impoverish the people that they would rise up and overthrow the existing order; but yet again, the prophets of doom have been confounded, for industrial society has invented ever fresh ways of reconciling its sometime disaffected masses to its changes and continuities.

This has been an extraordinary achievement; and the full cost of it is only now beginning to appear. For, in order to clasp its alienated and excluded to itself, industrialism was compelled to provide them with something of the privileges it had previously reserved only for a few. The only way to achieve this was through an enormous increase in production, which pressed into its service ever greater quantities of natural resources. The pollution which this created was at first seen as an acceptable by-product of an essentially happy state of affairs.

There had always been those who had deplored the despoiling of nature for industrial purposes, but they were seen merely as romantics, or, like contemporary Greens, accused of wanting to exclude the people from the benefits of industrialism, benefits of which they themselves took full advantage. 'It is not difficult to understand why protests against the destruction of nature became secondary; the more urgent issue of the existence of a menacing mass of poor and working-class people overshadowed what was considered a mere question of aesthetics. The internal threat to the growth and well-being of industrial society eclipsed what were seen as sentimental regrets over the impairment of the natural world.'[16]

It is the very success of this reconciliation that is now being celebrated throughout the Western world. The supreme claim of the West is that it can make its people happy, can give them all the good things of life, can render any desire for anything different both unnecessary and perverse. This has been the great conjuring trick underlying illusions about the end of history, to have spirited away the costs of this great reconciliation; costs which scarcely appear to the parties to it, those sometime adversaries called capital and labour.

What now threatens the system is an invasion of its sanctuaries in the West by all the accumulated costs involved in its solutions to the problems it has itself created. To believe that the industrial way of life can itself provide an answer from within, when its whole existence has been spent externalising its costs and its destructive capacity, requires a leap of faith which only the most spiritually robust would contemplate. The teeth of the troublesome dragon of labour were drawn, but where they fell, other, even more intractable monsters sprang up.

In this twilight time, we must therefore both await the retributive visitations created by costs elided in the past, and hope for deliverance from them. This is scarcely a rational expectation, even though it is produced by a view of the world which imagines itself to be guided by reason and common sense in all its actions. For in no other area of experience do we learn that we can really escape the consequences of our own actions, although from time to time, we may hope to get away with it. How is it possible that we should have been encouraged in such wanton irresponsibility to believe that even at this late hour, something will surely turn up? Perhaps we hope for another miracle from the same source which has produced so many economic wonders from a system which has constantly surprised its critics by its *resourcefulness*; a resourcefulness which has its origin in an abuse of resources, planetary and human.

But we still hope against hope that everything will turn out all right, that the worst won't happen, that we'll be let off the hook. Secretly, we believe that our children, or our children's children, will find the way forward; after all, look how much we've done for them, what we've lavished upon them, what resources we've put at their disposal. The future has, after all, been our reason for living, our consolation and confirmation, and how can we believe that so beneficent a force could possibly turn against us, could even, one fine day, fail us? The shining imagery of the future has been offered to us for so long that it has come to feel dependable, a faithful friend. How many times have we invoked future generations, tomorrow's world, posterity, those who will come after, the inheritors of a better world, the life hereafter, which has conspicuously ceased to be celestial? We have lived for the better times that are always to come, for the far horizons, for the coming attractions, for those happy days which are, surely, just around the corner. This faith in the future has kept us going through the bad times, when the pressure of the present has weighed too heavily upon us.

The future, that site of our deliverance, has now become

a battleground: for there, we have dumped not only our best hopes, but also our worst fears, cast out from our present way of life. Just what form of struggle these irreconcilables, these warring factions, may engage in is scarcely to be contemplated.

9

FINDING A BALANCE

BOTH CONSERVATISM AND radicalism are necessary elements in any balanced relationship between humanity and the world. Continuity and change underlie both the natural world and all human societies, indeed all life. Because so many of both the continuities and the changes in our lives are given – growth, maturity and death – it is all the more important that we consider carefully those continuities and changes over which we may be able to exercise some measure of real influence. God knows, the realm of the necessary is extensive enough, without subsuming it into those small areas where we might actually have limited freedoms. If we were to make a moral critique of our society, if we wanted to identify that in it which is evil, this is the area on which we would focus. It is the need to distinguish and discriminate between that which is truly unalterable and that which can, with some difficulty, be modified, which must be the basis of a new balance between different versions of radicalism and conservatism.

But surely, we all know what radicalism and conservatism are. Do we merely want to play with words? Do our library shelves not sag with weighty books about the Meaning of Conservatism, the Radical Tradition, the Liberal Heritage? And is not our political life centred on parties that claim to represent these opposing viewpoints in the world, even though they seem to command the allegiance of decreasing numbers of real people? And isn't the cut and thrust of these principled debates critical evidence of the robustness of our democracy?

What would a new radicalism propose, now that all the great radical causes have been won? Whatever specific issues such a radicalism might espouse, it would refuse to allow itself to be caught up, overtaken, colonised, by the workings of a social economic system whose infinite capacity for absorption will only swallow them up in order to serve its own abiding continuities. It would resist being exploited for purposes that are not its own. It would demand a different kind of change and, in so doing, would find itself allied to a form of conservatism which was looking for a different kind of continuity. It would not be the continuity of system imposing its own changes, but a continuous valuing of what has endured, of what human beings have found worthy of conservation in their own lives.

The new radicalism is not an even more fundamental disruption in people's lives than those they have already seen. It is not something to be brought to the people from without. Nor is it a theory to be cast around for in distant places or dusty books; not the Great Idea, not the over-arching ideology, not even the aetiological myth. To be radical now is to resist the ever more invasive intrusions of a world system that can afford to leave nothing alone, but that must open up new pathways to profit deep in the still unexploited fastnesses of the heart, the secret depths of the psyche, even while it goes about its global privatisations. To be radical now is to say that we have had enough of the industrialisation of our humanity. To be radical now is to say we want to be left alone to determine our lives, to say that our needs are more important than the system's necessities.

In so far as radicalism now means to resist, it begins to discover its identity with those forms of conservatism that have been by-passed and discarded by an industrial development that finds nothing of value but that which can be priced. True radicals and true conservatives both know that there are things that are beyond price, and that this precious inheritance sustains us all. A conservatism that has thrown in its lot with universal market forces has lost its roots; and a radicalism that accepts the gratuitous tearing up of all that is rooted in human experience could have no idea where it is going.

One of the great historical ironies for those 'radicals' who can see nothing worthy of conservation in the social tradition from which they spring, is their unwitting collusion with a 'conservatism' that is prepared to jettison everything, not least that radical tradition itself. In this way, those who believe that the onward march of market forces can further values that came into the world precisely to challenge the hegemony of market forces, are likely to be doomed to further future disappointments.

The new conservatism and the new radicalism that we seek form a mirror image of their present manifestations within the industrial system; and similarly, the relationship between them. In the existing order, the apparent opposition of conservatism and radicalism conceals their common subordination. Both tend solely to a conserving of profit; and the means whereby this is attained is through continuous change and upheaval. The new forms would also have a common objective, the sustaining of life. To this purpose they would ask for the conserving of what succours us most in human experience and tradition, and the uprooting of that which is propelling us towards extinction; and that is, not only the monopoly of wealth and power by the rich, but also their inhuman definition of what it means to be rich.

The existing system has taken the word sustainability to its heart, and now employs it at every turn, but in a context which deprives it of its meaning. For sustainability is the most basic form of conservatism. It means not taking from the earth, from the world, from society, from each other, from life, more than we give back. But when industrial society uses the word, it means the sustaining of itself, no matter what the cost. It means sustaining privilege, sustaining poverty, sustaining abuse of the earth, sustaining inequality, sustaining starvation, sustaining violence. To sustain the existing system, to defend the status quo, is neither conservative nor sustainable. It is not even a status quo. For what is called the status quo is a form of continuous depletion, of entropy.

And such conservatism will perish if it is not subjected to a radical revaluation.

Here we see the fundamental contradiction of a conservatism that has attached itself to a system that subverts all values and practices that we want desperately to conserve. Those so-called conservatives who piously and ingenuously ask nothing more than to be allowed to continue with things as they are, to be permitted to maintain our tried and trusted ways of doing things, are actually grave-diggers, preparing for the funeral rites, not only of economic systems, but also of the earth itself. What a sad and bitter irony that those who were predicted to be the grave-diggers of capitalism, the Western working class, have become, to a considerable extent, the foot soldiers in this war against the planet.

Naturally, this new militant role has been hidden from the working class ('We have a right to what we've got'), as were their earlier roles in an exploitative system, as factory or cannon fodder, and equally in its projected overthrow, as the vanguard of history. We have constantly been pressed into the service of warmongers, whether the war of all against each, class war, or war against the planet, wars for the most part never formally declared, and prosecuted without consultation.

It would be a central characteristic of the new radicalism that the people should determine their own role and function in bringing about social change and safeguarding human continuities. This would necessarily require a keener recognition of the covert role we are playing in the current conflict over control of planetary resources. For once more, we find that the common people, the masses, the working classes, the popular forces, the rank and file, have been enlisted under false colours. And this time, it is a war even more dreadful than the ghastly conflicts which have preceded it.

Some might feel that such calls for the people to understand the role they are presently playing come perilously close to the old Marxist debate about false consciousness. But Marx's insights have not been invalidated by the downfall of Eastern European communism. After all, social injustice has not abated simply because state socialism has collapsed. On the contrary; its global exacerbation is essential to the success of the world economic system. To the extent that the Soviet power bloc inhibited this process, its removal is doubtless a cause for rejoicing in the West. The West no longer sees any opposition to intensifying inequalities; and because it does not have to contend with even the pretence of a different way of life based on Marxism, it does not have to take seriously the arguments of Marx.

In this it is almost certainly mistaken. There is a case to be made – and indeed, people, not theorists, are making it – that many of Marx's prophecies have already been realised, although unremarked upon by the West. The people living in the slums of the cities of Brazil, who must deal daily with the mutilations and murders of organised crime, slum bosses and drug wars, say that Marx's prediction that we would have to choose between socialism or barbarism has already come true. 'We have barbarism here and now. It isn't in the future. We are living it each day.'[17]

The truth is that popular consciousness is always dual and shifting, not to say ambiguous. For people are supremely aware of the benefits of industrialism, to which, in their long history, they have been rather recently admitted, and for which they may feel the gratitude that is natural in those who have been for so long excluded from the feast. There is nothing false about this consciousness. But there is also another, growing consciousness, which is equally real, and which involves a developing awareness of the dangerous consequences of precisely that industrial way of life which provides those benefits. The only falsity in these conflicting consciousnesses is that they can be painlessly reconciled. The falsest consciousness of all would be to believe that we can go on as we are.

The new friends of the people who tell us that we can have it all, are actually the enemies of the earth; and how can anyone who is an enemy of the earth be a friend to humankind? The people need neither friends nor enemies. What they do need is to rely on themselves and to trust one another. It is time to break with the others who know it all, the experts and professionals, the advisers, the leaders, the wise men, the guides, the guardians, all those who would tell us that we do not, and cannot understand. For who can claim to be an expert in telling us how to live our human lives?

It is not easy to value our own insights against the confident certainties of the experts. We are constantly told that we live in the most complex and advanced societies that the world has ever known, and that it is impossible for a mere individual to comprehend anything but the most minute portion of that reality which falls within her immediate competence. They tell us this is an information-rich society, which even the latest generation of computers can barely contain within their storehouse of memory. We are taught that we are now all members of a single global system, over which even nation states can have little influence; what influence could we, as individuals, have over such unbiddable forces?

Social complicatedness is not the same as complexity; indeed, our complex society is far more simple than those who complicate it would have us perceive. Its underlying dynamics are elegantly simple: they serve to concentrate wealth and power where these are already abundant. Of course, in order to achieve these simple ends, the most elaborate structures and convoluted processes have been developed. Why else would giant trucks ply the motorways of Europe, bringing products which could more cheaply and easily be made in the place where they are to be consumed? Why otherwise would we be required to buy biscuits from Germany, coal from South Africa, matches from Czechoslovakia, yoghurt from France, underpants from Taiwan, shirts from Thailand, carnations from Israel? This complex international division of labour all tends to the same single and simple end.

Faced with these underlying simplicities, there is one simple question to be asked. Since we cannot go on as we are, and since any alternative is unthinkable, what are we going to do? This ought to be the subject, the central question of contemporary politics, as well as the focus of all our social concerns. Caught up in the answer we give is our children's future, the purposes of our labour, the shape of our common life, the way we answer our deepest needs, the very meaning we give to our existence.

We are reluctant even to frame this question, let alone to seek an answer. What we fear most is not that our relationship with the planet might be revealed – most of us know that already – but that the nature of our relationship with the system would be laid bare; and that would be intolerable. Such genuinely political discussions remain tentative, arcane, specialised, awkward. They are banished from the mainstream, because the economic system is always given precedence over the planet. Wealth is believed to be more important than life.

We have been invited to the feast, but a little too late. We have arrived in time to witness the orgiastic climax. It is now beginning to dawn on us that it is we who will have to pick up the tab, if indeed, it is payable in any coinage we possess.

10

THE CLOSED CIRCLE

IF SUCH FUNDAMENTAL questions are not even asked, this is because well-rehearsed answers to them already exist. Common wisdom assures us in a hundred familiar saws and aphorisms that 'you can't change the world'.

Whose voice is speaking through these weary self-protective phrases? Perhaps we are dealing with a sagacious recognition of our human limitations. Or are we merely hearing the limits of the possible, which one particular society imposes upon its people?

We wonder whether we are in the presence of a universal human condition, or of a society whose universalising pretensions lead it to make false claims for what is only its own arbitrary value-system. Perhaps the beliefs and structures of Western society have become so powerful that we come to believe that these mark the boundaries of human existence itself. The social has colonised the existential. This is nothing new, though the claim of any localised society to be the cosmos is usually associated with what the West has labelled 'primitive societies'. We smile sadly when we read that the Sioux imagined that their ghost dance would resuscitate all their dead, who would come to their help in fighting off the assault of the white man. We marvel at the ability of so many tiny groups to construct a universe of which they are invariably the centre, and on whose local mountains the gods of the universe have their habitation. That the advanced societies of the West, with all their sophistications, are as securely and self-confidently installed within the same fiduciary construct, is curiously beyond imagination. What we

101

are doing is precisely what we observe lesser peoples to have done. It seems that, after all, there are no primitive societies; or, if there are, the West is certainly among them.

Once located within a society, no one can know for certain where the alterable finishes and the unalterable begins in human existence. What we can be clear about is that all societies strive to make absolute claims for the contingent, for the socially determined, and present these as necessary and inescapable, and, more often than not, as divinely ordained. Those who exhort us to live in the real world, to acknowledge the facts of life, to come down to earth, speak as though they were enunciating truths brought back from the beyond, the sacred formulae on which the moral order of the universe rests; those creaking pillars of decaying faith in yet another totalising ideology.

It is not surprising that people so readily accept the way things are, the socially given, because these do merge imperceptibly with those things that are truly given – the central realities of birth, growth, ageing and death. A strong society is one which manages to convey to those it shelters some sense of universal necessity, however parochial and local the social arrangements may actually be. And the more effectively a society transmits its system of beliefs to individuals, the more fortified those individuals will be against any disconfirming experience, and the more readily they'll name strangers as infidels, aliens, heretics, unbelievers, as outlandish and uncivilised.

Western society has been particularly successful in this endeavour, because it has been the most powerful and irresistible colonising force in the world, and continues to be so. Its eager incursion into the vacant ideological spaces of Eastern Europe is only the most recent of its imperial adventures. Sixty years ago, the anthropologist Ruth Benedict had already described this process:

> Western civilization, because of fortuitous historical circumstances, has spread itself more widely than any other local group that has so far been known. It has standardized itself over most of the globe, and we have been led, therefore, to

102

accept a belief in the uniformity of human behaviour that under other circumstances would not have arisen. Even very primitive peoples are sometimes far more conscious of the role of cultural traits than we are, and for good reason. They have had intimate experience of different cultures. They have seen their religion, their economic system, their marriage prohibitions, go down before the white man's. They have laid down the one and accepted the other, often uncomprehendingly enough, but they are quite clear that there are variant arrangements of human life . . .

The psychological consequences of this spread of white culture have been out of all proportion to the materialistic. This worldwide cultural diffusion has protected us as man has never been protected before from having to take seriously the civilizations of other peoples; it has given to our culture a massive universality that we have long ceased to account for historically, and which we read off rather as necessary and inevitable. We interpret our dependence, in our civilization, upon economic competition, as proof that this is the prime motivation that human nature can rely on, or we read off the behaviour of small children as it is moulded in our civilization and recorded in child clinics, as child psychology, or the way in which the young human animal is bound to behave. It is the same whether it is a question of our ethics or of our family organization. It is the inevitability of each familiar motivation that we defend, attempting always to identify our local ways of behaving with Behaviour, or our own socialized habits with Human Nature.[18]

The missionising expansionism of the West, far from coming to an end at the formal close of the colonial era in the Fifties and Sixties, actually intensified. The means of control were no longer born through military conquest and occupation of the territory of others, but had to find other, less tangible, forms of domination. The economic ideology of the West became the source of its continuing dominion, which it imposed upon the rest of the world. This enterprise was made more plausible by the spectacular post-war prosperity in the West. It is an historic irony that the wealth of the West depended to such a degree upon exploitation of those very territories now enjoined to imitate its example.

The capture and control by the West of global economic resources has underpinned its remorseless insistence that it alone was right. The dissolution of those societies in Eastern Europe which claimed to live on a different economic and moral basis has given the apparently final vindication to these grandiose claims. If there is a tendency in every society to universalise its particular world view, how much stronger must this become when those who gaze outwards from its inner fastness see everything fall before its proclaimed truths. Strength has often been mistaken for truth, and when the whole world seems ready to prostrate itself before this revelation, who, living at the heart of this benign imperium, would be so foolish as to flirt with the disgraced heresies of doomed societies?

So secure is the West in its unalterable necessity, that it is able to offer its people, not rituals of obedience to its own compulsions, but on the contrary, something which it calls 'freedom of choice'. In fact, making choices is at the very heart of the proclaimed values of our 'pluralistic society'. These choices appear to range from selecting products in the marketplace, to opting for a particular lifestyle, as well as the sacred right to believe anything you like. It is these freedoms which distinguish us from those less fortunate peoples who are in thrall to superstition or ideology or other constraining beliefs. The West thus offers a most happy contrast to the discredited creed of communism, to the formless polytheism of precolonial peoples, or to the ghoulish excesses of Islam. Faith itself in the West is seen as a matter of personal preference, and is not to be imposed by any priesthood, religious or secular. We do not have to commit ourselves to any ceremonies of faith or rituals of belief; we may occasionally be asked to state, especially at significant moments in our lives, such as applying for new jobs or going into hospital, our spiritual status. The proudest boast of the West is that it constitutes a secular, rational society.

This self-description is simply untrue. The only difference between the West and other non-secular, non-rational societies, is that it demands its tribute of faith in areas of human experience other than those traditionally associated with religion. The apparent tolerance of diversity and choice and freedom have to be paid for, not in the nebulous realm of belief, but in practice. People are free to believe anything they want, but what is absolutely required is that they live and behave in ways that are profitable, not, of course, to their immortal souls, but to that social and economic system which has profit as its deepest and most unalterable purpose. We should not be deceived by the glittering array of choices: they are conditional. You can indeed have what you want, as long as what you want is available; what is available is what is market-worthy; what is not available on these terms ceases to exist. The very quantity of what is on offer distracts us from what isn't. Much of this has been taken off the market, apparently for lack of demand, or is otherwise out of stock. In any case, much of it is obsolete, yesterday's merchandise, shop-soiled, could find no buyer. In any case, such items were insubstantial, abstract, entities of dubious existence, even though in some other societies they might have been regarded as classical freedoms, too precious to be left to the mercies of the retail outlet. Among them we might count freedom from insecurity, freedom from fear, freedom from isolation, freedom from a restless and objectless wanting.

What other choices are we left with in Western society than choosing from the preselected commodities that crowd the marketplace? Of course, not to consume remains a theoretical choice, but not to buy is to move out of the culture, to pass into exile. Those who exercise such freedoms can be found doing so in cardboard boxes and shop doorways and under the bridges of the great cities. If we cannot choose to provide for our own need, if we have no control over the production or provenance of what we eat, or where we live, or how we work, or what purposes that work serves, or to lead a life that is good rather than the 'good life' as defined by market values, then some very fundamental choices have been suppressed. In the absence of such choices, are we, too, not living under a total system, the success of which has been apparently to render alternatives, at least for a time, both superfluous and unattainable?

What common sense we display in our dutiful acceptance of what we can have; what prudent forbearance we show in not venturing on to the quicksands of forbidden territory, where the NO TRESPASSING signs fence off a derelict private property that is home for our vagrant needs and wandering desires. When there is so much that is available, why repine for what has been placed off limits? If we persist, we shall be told in no uncertain manner that this is all there is, that we are beating the bounds of human possibilities, when we are merely pressing against the perimeter fences erected by authority for the defence of its realm.

Perhaps, after all, the most powerful achievement of the rich Western societies is this: to have transformed society into existence. The world they have made has become the only world that is. Such a recognition is implicit, when people say 'What else is there?' 'You've got to live in the real world'; everywhere else is cloud-cuckoo land, an impossible utopia, a fool's paradise.

It is the absence of any other imaginable world which attaches people to this one with all the more urgency. If this is the only reality, what possible other reaction could we have than a determination to get all we can out of it while we are here? This is the translation, at the level of felt experience, of the underlying economic compulsion. So you have to live life to the full, get it while it's going, milk it for all it's worth, get some of the action, not miss out on your share, live for today, go for it, squeeze it dry. 'I want it all and I want it now' becomes the only rational response to the only world that there is, the only world there could be; and indeed nothing could be worse than the thought of leaving it, whether for an after-life or for a better life in the here and now.

Traditional cosmologies are turned upside down. If there is no heaven to go to, this doesn't matter because we shall require no compensation for joys foregone here below. In such a blissful state, is it any wonder that death should be so terrible, and even the thought of it forbidden? That you can't take it with you becomes no longer a prudent admonition against an over-attachment to the things of this world (why would anybody ever have worried about that?), but rather the terrified cry of a derelict humanity abandoned by all meaning. This fear becomes, in turn, a good reason for falling upon the good things of life with even more ferocious appetite (in economic terms, consuming more). If our needs are no longer earthly, but have become the stuff of transcendence, what does it matter if we devour the earth?

So it is that even our consciousness of the irremediable – the certainty of suffering, the necessity of death – no longer serves as a basis for religion or a support for moral philosophy. On the contrary, this consciousness is actually exploited to chain us more securely to the socially determined: and we are then ready to be led to market, to seek such meaning, solace and spiritual consolation as may be obtained there.

Of course, what can't be remedied in human life has always been dressed up with social meaning. Death, disease, loss, madness, suffering – these have always had a message for us. These inescapable visitations have never stood as themselves, never appeared naked, but have always been invested with such meanings as would validate the existing social order. But there is a crucial difference. Where once these afflictions were used by the priests to imbue people with restraint, caution, self-control, and the need to pay attention to their immortal soul, they are now employed to inculcate the opposites – a frenzy of living for the present, an orgy of taking all that is on offer, an urgency of seizing life with both hands. Here, we come close to what are the religious roots of a society which proclaims its secular nature, and its emancipation from all forms of superstition. Those who have detected something reminiscent of the imagery of the Middle Ages in contemporary life – its squalors, violence, crazes and wonders, in the taste for miracles, its plagues and fairs, its peddlars and beggars, its freak shows and performances – may have sensed something of the underlying hysterias of our age; we are after all living in a medieval allegory, in which good and evil have been simply repainted in the garish primary colours of wealth and poverty.

The desire for immediate pleasure is not, of course, peculiar to our own culture, or restricted to our own time. There have always been those in all societies who have exhorted us to 'eat, drink and be merry for tomorrow we die'. But this has hitherto remained a seditious and heretical view of human purposes. It has now become the dominant injunction, the imperative even, of Western society. It is now philosophy, religion, reflection, contemplation which have become the heresies, the austere luxuries which cannot be afforded by the richest societies of the world.

Of course, the unavoidable pain and suffering of life have always had to be sweetened. We have merely substituted the consolations of consumerism for the comforts of religion. What it might mean to face life without any such supports, we find it hard to imagine, but we may have to try.

However difficult it may be to put into words, there is a human solidarity, a spontaneous responsiveness to need which requires no justification beyond itself, something which the moment of need calls into being. When an elderly woman falls in the street, she is not simply left to lie there. When a train crashes, people do not have to be told what to do, but tear away at the wreckage with their bare hands. George Eliot, as she sought to elaborate her religion of humanity, writes of a deathbed scene in *Scenes of Clerical Life*:

> No wonder the sick room and the lazar house have so often been a refuge from the tossings of intellectual doubt – a place of repose for the worn and wounded spirit. Here is a duty about which all creeds and philosophies are as one: here, at least, the conscience will not be dogged by doubt, the benign impulse will not be checked by adverse theory; here you may begin to act without settling one preliminary question ... Where a human being lies prostrate, thrown on the tender mercies of his fellow, the moral relation of man to man is reduced to its utmost clearness and simplicity; bigotry cannot confuse it, theory cannot pervert it, passion, awed into acquiescence, can neither pollute nor perturb it.[19]

These generous impulses are deformed when human suffering is used to invoke the workings of divine purpose; they are no less so when suffering is exploited to goad people on to consume, to fulfil those economic purposes which have become, strangely, the sole expression of the beyond in our midst, our only means of transcendence. We are bound to ask whether there could exist any more effective solace than that which either religion, or its bastard offspring, consumerism, can provide. The courage to respond adequately to suffering must come from the recognition that suffering can be neither transcended nor bought off. How far such courage is possible is a question we must go on asking. One thing we can say is that an economic system which identifies its own necessities with the limits of existence is forced to ignore such questions.

However, the suppression of such questions does not mean that they or their consequences disappear from the world. On the contrary. They return to haunt the consciousness of individuals, who then are forced to ask them in rhetorical and uncomprehending pain 'Why me? Why does this terrible illness, this unbearable bereavement, happen to me?' 'Why should I be the one to suffer?' 'What have I done to deserve this?' In this way, experiences which might once have been regarded as common and inevitable, even perhaps as part of the burden of our common humanity, have been degraded, transformed into sterile and depressing personal misfortunes. The most that can be hoped for from society is mitigation in the only form it knows – insurance payments, damages, compensation; and distractions – don't think about it, don't brood, put it behind you, pick up the pieces and get on with your life.

Yet the fundamental conditions of life give rise to these deep anguishes and achings; and they are incurable. What is happening is that society claims to be able to cure what is without remedy, whereas in fact what it is really doing is submerging its own contradictions in the cures it purports to offer. These derisory specifics only add to the burden that we all have to carry, but which we do not have to bear alone. In other words, the salvation promised is an illusion: we cannot escape our human limitations. The pretence that we can only compounds our unhappiness, and renders invisible to us the real, but modest mitigations that we can offer each other.

11

HUMAN NATURE

PERHAPS THE MOST important obstacle to the development of a new radicalism is the ideology of human nature.

Any discussion, no matter how exploratory, about the possibility of social change is very quickly inhibited by the conclusive and terminal argument that 'You can't change human nature'. This has become a blunt weapon for laying into even the most tentative discussions of how things might be other than they are. The sentence is uttered as a final judgement. Those who pronounce it do so with a grim satisfaction which places them among the knowing of the world, those for whom the universe holds no further mysteries.

It should not surprise us too much if a society that has colonised existence gives back the result of its work as 'human nature', thereby disowning any responsibility for what is in fact its most characteristic product. The very insistence that human nature cannot be changed could equally well be an indication of the contrary: that human nature has already proved itself to be all too malleable. Why else would it have congealed so easily into the arbitrary one-dimensional shape we now observe? What seems to have happened is that an extraordinarily powerful society has produced, and then legitimated, certain restricted forms of behaviour, and has then declared them to be both unalterable and quintessentially human. No higher degree of social perfection could be imagined. The engineers of human souls employed by other totalitarian ideologies were, by contrast, crude mechanics.

When people declare with such authority that human nature cannot be changed, they are rarely challenged. So we never find out what they are really saying. Do they mean that this social and economic order is in fact a kind of outcrop of human nature, its direct and effective expression, its simple embodiment? Or do they mean that the plasticity of human nature has lent itself so completely and unresistingly to the shapings required by the social order that we can no longer recognise their separateness? Or do they mean that they don't want society changed because they feel their interests are well protected by the way things are?

In spite of the strength of these statements, there is a curious narrowness and selectivity about the idea of what constitutes human nature. When people insist that human nature cannot be changed, they rarely mean that you cannot prevent people from demonstrating their spontaneous idealism, or from rushing to help those involved in an accident, or struggling for justice against the overwhelming wisdom of those who know better. If it wasn't human nature that drove a young Chinese student to dance alone in front of the advancing tanks in Tiananmen Square, then what was it? Was Nelson Mandela's nature less or more than human when he kept faith and retained his dignity through a quarter of a century on Robben Island? Was there something inhuman in the resistance of Chico Mendes to those invading the rainforest?

But the defenders of the unchangeability of human nature are unlikely to be persuaded by these, or by any number of examples that run counter to their conviction. This is because they are not really interested in human nature at all; but they are extremely concerned about the nature of the social and economic system which serves them so well. We should not fool ourselves that we are in the presence of a serious debate about what human life is really all about; we are face to face with an ideological construct. Thus it is that when these realists of human nature come to the conclusion that human beings are basically, essentially, unalterably greedy, selfish, short-sighted, venal, rapacious, competitive, their version of human nature exhibits a singular congruence with the essential requirements of the capitalist system.

Why is this thin account of reality so readily accepted as

the last word? Why do those who are most unhappy with its implications nevertheless feel impotent against its force? Why do so many hopeful radicalisms falter and withdraw under its withering blast?

One fundamental reason is that, like so much in our secular society, the human nature argument takes a borrowed, but now suppressed, authority from the Christian story of the Fall. Human nature is not only fallen, but it fell a long time ago. Human depravity, wickedness, sinfulness, have been a constant theme in a civilisation which has always had pretensions to universality, but which only in the past 500 years has had the means to enforce it. Thus it is that the ghost of Christian doctrine still haunts the empty house of the modern secular world. However, there is a vital departure from the tradition. Human nature is not invoked as a prelude to redemption, or to any other spiritual consolation, but is presented as a hard, brutal, unavoidable truth, political and existential.

This dogma of human nature is indeed the liberator of energies, forces, desires which are required to fuel the engines of capitalist growth. Its exalted function is now to vindicate those sins that were once imprisoned in profitless religious prohibitions. The historian R. H. Tawney pointed out, in *Religion and the Rise of Capitalism*, that what in medieval Christendom had been denounced as the vices of greed, selfishness and covetousness, were transformed by capitalist society into the virtues of enterprise, initiative and accumulation.

Since the early industrial period, this process has intensified and deepened. The vices-become-virtues have now become indispensable to the constantly expanding universe of capitalist activity. They now dominate human behaviour, compel people to act in particular ways, and are then rationalised as the promptings of an unalterable human nature. Indeed, these vices-become-virtues have become so deeply rooted in the psychological as well as in the social sub-systems of the West that something of the moral ambiguities surrounding them can be admitted once more. No longer do we need to pretend, like the early Puritans, that these forms of behaviour are unalloyed shining virtues; they simply, irredeemably, exist. In our better moments, we might even deplore them, wish it were otherwise; but a moment's reflection tells us that it would be unthinkable to curb or attempt to reform those appetites that bring to life the forces slumbering in the lap of nature. A malleable humanity is the raw material out of which the market economy has fashioned its human nature.

Thus, there even persists a sense of failed idealism behind the assertion that human nature is unchangeable – though perhaps it is no longer accessible to those who use the axiom most emphatically. Indeed, this suppressed idealism is a pallid afterglow of both Christian hopes and of their more secular expression in socialist visions. For if Christianity insisted on the wretchedness and depravity of human nature, this was only in order to illuminate, by contrast, the redemptive possibilities through which that human nature could be transformed. And if socialists saw capitalism as fostering only the worst and most corrupt aspects of human nature, this was in order to celebrate the positive qualities that people nevertheless exhibited, in spite of oppression and exploitation, human qualities which would attain their fullest flowering under the socialism that was to come.

With what exuberance and delight have the proponents of the human-nature argument welcomed the failure of socialism in Eastern Europe. See, they say, how eager people are to tear down the creaking structures of the command economies, and to embrace the liberating promises of the market economy. This is because the cowed and captive peoples of the East have always wanted what we've got. This is human nature, they continue, not in theory, but in practice. The great lie of the perfectibility of humanity has been shown up as the delusion it is. What we saw was a mass conversion to the basic tenets of Western ideology, as millions celebrated their rebirth into a new life. How significant that this emancipated human nature, which always hankers after freedom, so eagerly grasped the only version of freedom that was available. For among the variegated merchandise on display in the supermarkets of the West, there is, apparently, unlike washing powder or cat food, only one brand of freedom.

Perhaps the most damaging effect of the human-nature argument is that it effectively denies the real ambiguities in human experience. Of course this sombre and bleak view of human nature has also called forth its opposite. It has been the error of too many would-be reformers to postulate its bright mirror image, to insist on the fundamental goodness of human nature, which is vitiated by wicked social arrangements. Once these were changed, it was confidently held, the reign of universal love and harmony would begin.

Powerful ideologies always summon their shadows, define their own opposites. One extreme conjures up its other. Measure and balance, the tolerance of complexity are lost. Thus, instead of postulating the fundamental goodness of human nature against its unalterable depravity, what we require is an understanding of its essential ambiguities, and the way these are shaped by arbitrary social structures. This would be a more valuable starting point, both for a genuine exploration of human nature, as well as of the nature of society. Why are we so reluctant to admit ambivalences and contradictions? Why do the ideologies insist on such caricatures of our humanity? Is it because, were they to concede something of the complexity, the subtleties, the diversity of our human natures, alternative ways of living, or different kinds of changing, might appear more plausible?

If the human-nature dogma elicits general assent, this could be because we can all discover the affirming evidence for it within ourselves. We all know at what depths our capacity for greed, deception, envy, ruthlessness operate. Only we know how cruel we can be. However, rather than conceding that this is the final confirmation of the correctness of the ideology, it might be more significant to ask how it has come about that so partial and one-sided an account of the human heart has gained ascendancy. Whatever has happened to us? How have we been led, browbeaten, coerced into accepting this version of ourselves as some kind of final truth?

We can perhaps best understand this as a form of colonisation. If the power and might of the West could so easily open a passage for its ideas and values in its subject peoples, why should we imagine that we should be proof against such processes? We have seen all other values go down before this invasive power, all other systems of knowledge and patterns of behaviour wiped out. In the occupied territories, anything that does not correspond to the ways of the victors must either go underground or perish. We, who are at the heart of the imperialist West, have also been colonised. That it began with industrialism itself should not obscure the fact that it continues, develops and deepens through time. Who has colonised us? We have been colonised by the superior power of wealth and its reasons. Money, like the heart, has its reasons which reason knoweth not.

The march of colonialism has always involved, first the inferiorising, and then the eclipse of the local, the traditional and the familiar. It imposes, usually by force, its own, alien version of the world. When people can no longer see in the dominant culture any confirmation of what they know, their own knowledge comes to seem increasingly tenuous and unreal. Sometimes, it goes underground, and creates the subterranean energies that fuel resistance movements and liberation struggles. This was the response provoked in the Third World by the first colonising attempts by the West. The lesson has been well taken. A more sophisticated colonialism has learnt not only a more subtle form of dominance, but it also promises its own version of liberation – the prospect of endless wealth. This is known to work, because it has been tried and tested in what are sometimes called the metropolitan countries.

Indeed, we in the West, have been in the forefront of this colonisation. We have seen our instincts for generosity, altruism, compassion and solidarity disgraced, made to seem unreal and foolish. In the end, we come to collude with the public suppression of these qualities, and begin to agree that they have no place in the way we must now live. We accept that these virtues must be confined to a shrunken domain, restricted to our private lives – the family, personal relationships, friendships. We are then destined to discover that these privatised spheres are not so separate after all, but are increasingly contaminated by the dominant values which refuse to observe the frontiers we have erected. We flee from the cruelties of our social existence into the fortress of our private refuge, only to find there further refinements of those horrors we thought we had escaped.

The most widespread reaction to these invasive processes has been the growth of a general cynicism. When we want to argue with the occupying powers, we find it hard to resist their propaganda, because, when we look inside ourselves, we discern there that all-too-corrupt nature which they have preached to us in their diabolic sermons. After all, to be honest, aren't we all greedy, venal, on the make, out for number one? Isn't our eye always fixed firmly on the main chance, isn't something for nothing the sweetest of daily victories when we return home with our booty, the day's pickings, which we are told is the reward for our labours? Do not even the poets admit that when we turn our gaze inwards, what we shall observe is 'The foul smithy of the human heart'?

It is all such a revelation. Under the skin, we are all the same. This is what unites us, a negative solidarity of cynical knowingness. Of course there's nothing wrong with the social order, that wise and beneficent dispensation. It's us. It is we who are unworthy. The fault is in us. How naïve, how foolish were those who lived in a less disillusioned age, those who imagined that there was even a possibility that we might be anything other than the poor naked animals we so clearly are. How privileged we are, that it has been granted to us to discover the truth of the human condition. This is progress.

This view is not just popular myth, but is supported by much academic research, which confirms the extent of the selfishness, violence and malevolence of an unregenerate humanity. Every day brings fresh evidence. Yesterday we learned that the abuse of children is more widespread than we had ever dreamed; today that incest psychologically disables thousands; tomorrow we shall hear that crimes of violence against the person have reached unprecedented levels. However sensitively the research is carried out, and however altruistic the motivations of the researchers, these findings will be eagerly seized upon by the enthusiastic demolitionists of human solidarities, and set before us triumphantly as the ultimate revelations of our depraved nature.

The aggregate of all such findings has the effect of increasing discord and mistrust between people. Bonds of kinship, ties of blood, all sympathies and affinities, are weakened. Should we discern in the deployment of these findings a concern for human well-being, or the furthering of an individualism so extreme that it would have us believe that all relationships, bondings and solidarities are doomed to collapse in betrayal and acrimony? It seems that the last thing we can expect of one another, even of these we have taken to be our nearest and dearest, is that we can offer each other shelter and succour, the consolation of staying together in a world increasingly inhabited by 'monsters', 'beasts' and 'fiends'? (The researchers do not use this language, of course, but the popular press has fewer inhibitions, and takes up the theme with greater gusto and intemperance.)

We might wonder why the chroniclers of human disgrace, and those whose melancholy function it is to formulate social policy in response to their findings, so rarely undertake research into the social structuring of these individual pathologies. To ascribe, for example, the injuries of women and children to something called 'male violence' or 'sexism' is to explain nothing at all; worse, it reinforces the ideology of an unchangeable male (human) nature. It is our willingness to rest in such fatalistic universalisms that inhibits further scrutiny of a society which has reached such an 'advanced' stage.

Of course, anyone who deliberately sought to conceal or cover up the horrors of which human beings are undoubtedly capable, would in no way be serving humanity. But underlying this ever-extending disclosure of mistreatment and brutality, there lies an assumption that we have unveiled a final, irreducible revelation about 'human nature'. What we need to understand is that this is a product, not of truth, but of ideology. In other words, the driving asunder of human associations and solidarities is the consequence of an ideology that requires the separation and isolation of people one from another.

How could it be that something essential about ourselves

is being disclosed by such research? What we are seeing is, rather, the consequence of centuries of the single-minded development of very specific aspects of human nature (and the rigorous suppression of others) in pursuit of economic gain.

The abuse of children, violence against women, the acts of cruelty and betrayal occur, for the most part, in that depleted place called the family. These things are a consequence of the depopulating of the heart, yet another shift of population, in order to make room for the plethora of marketed goods and services that must make their home there. There has been a clearance sale of humanity, a mass exodus from the psychic spaces, where those closest to us have become objects of suspicion, where the ties of kinship have been loosened, the most primary affections prised apart. We must learn, to our own wonderment and fear, that we really are on our own now. In place of those primitive, archaic associations which we might once have cherished, we are offered as a substitute constant renewal, a perpetual celebration of all that money will provide us with. This is the pathological dynamic that has been set up, whereby, for the sake of economic improvements, everything else is thrown away on to the rising garbage heaps of waste, which are among the most conspicuous ornaments of our culture. This deviancy was once labelled idolatry, but it has now been normalised to such a degree that those who seek to resist it are called bleeding hearts, weak-minded sentimentalists, nostalgics stranded in time, not living in that real world of disorder and violence which is our natural element, our home.

The continuing drama of outrages against the weakest and most vulnerable has become a rolling media spectacle; from child prostitution to drugs, from alcohol abuse to glue-sniffing, from addiction to gambling to rising crime; the half million telephone calls to the Samaritans each year, the alcohol abuse that fills one hospital bed in five, assaults upon the elderly – all these things are, in large measure, socially produced. The production of unhappiness is one of the most profitable enterprises of post-industrial societies. Indeed, the mills and factories which create expensive forms of distress and new lines in value-added misery, are working as never before.

If only some of the funding devoted to the lugubrious uncovering of our fallen state could be diverted into investigations of the relationship between the creation of wealth and the conspicuous forms of suffering that attend it, there might be more help for the injured humanity that fills the doctors' surgeries, the air space and advice columns and the consulting rooms of therapists, that seeks shelter in cardboard boxes under bridges, or that cries itself to sleep in the luxury house where the nearest neighbours are far beyond shouting distance.

12

WHY HUMAN NATURE CANNOT BE CHANGED

ONCE THIS BLEAK view of human nature is accepted, paradoxically, human nature ceases to be a problem. Once we acknowledge that things are as they are, and there is no point in struggling against them, there is an enormous sense of relief. The burden is lifted from our shoulders, not because of the pilgrim's salvation or redemption, but because the delights of Vanity Fair far outweigh our inevitable sorrows. In this way, we can relax, and enjoy every novelty, every new sensation, every fresh experience, every acquisition, which then become a confirmation of the wisdom of having submitted ourselves so wholeheartedly to that happy reality which, by coincidence, is both our fate on earth and our social destiny.

Having decreed the immutable depravities of human nature, the capitalist system then, with mysterious magnanimity, takes them to its bosom, swallows them whole and spews them forth as noble virtues. The earliest expositors of the dogma of political economy made it clear that it was 'not from the benevolence of the butcher, the brewer, or the baker that we expect our dinner, but from their regard to their own interest. We address ourselves, not to their humanity, but to their self-love, and never talk to them of our own necessities, but of their advantages. Nobody but a beggar chooses to depend chiefly upon the benevolence of his fellow-citizens.'[20] The capitalist creed then declares that it alone can give free expression to the most baleful of human energies in such a way that they will not damage others, as they would surely do if left unattended. As it is, the most destructive of human

passions expend themselves harmlessly in the obscure laby-
rinth of political economy, and emerge above ground only
in the sunny avocations of counting house and marketplace.

What could possibly be more utopian than this 'real
world', in which private vice is so effortlessly transformed
into public virtue? Given the level of credulity that modern
economics demands, it becomes clear that all the assertions
that human nature cannot be changed actually mean something else: that human nature *must* not be changed. For
capitalism requires that human nature remain unchanged
within the limitations it has itself imposed, and banishes all
the positive characteristics of that nature into a private exile
of personal charity, love, kindness, familial sentiment – where
they will do no harm to that supreme good which depends
upon the subterranean vices undergoing their mysterious
work of transvaluation. It clearly will not do to ponder too
deeply on this process. We might speculate that the division
of labour is not confined to the material world, but operates
with equal efficacy in the realm of morality. Or perhaps we
discern here the guiding hand of Providence. This is the true
economic miracle. What earlier ages had feared as uncontrollable vices have become domesticated through the workings
of political economy, tamed like animals culled from the wild,
and their energies harnessed for the sake of their productive
power. Few have noticed the boldness of the assertion that
where world religions had failed in the management of a
wayward humanity, the ingenious arrangements of the
economists might succeed. 'Poor sillie Church of Christ,'
exclaimed Tawney's seventeenth-century Anglican divine,
'that could never finde a lawful usurie before this golden age
wherein we live.'

But we are told that an even greater miracle than this
awaits us. We are expected to believe that these raw passions,
constantly excited and inflamed, will accept docile confinement in the public realm. Alas, when we look more closely
at the private sphere, not in the pages of the standard texts
of economic theory, but in the lived relations of contemporary life, we look in vain. What we see are separations, discon-
tent, ruptured ties, dispersals, strife, bitterness, recrimination,

anger. But, we will be told, these are merely individual problems, the difficulties of all human lives. Such things exist in all societies, independently of the workings of social and economic systems.

Is this true? It is undeniable that suffering and unkindness are present in all societies. But it is possible to conceive that there might be societies which would do their best to assuage such suffering, and to mitigate unkindness; just as we know that there are societies – one, at least – which exacerbate and make use of them. Indeed, when a society has a vested interest in the exploitation of suffering and unkindness, it will be tempted to prolong and intensify them, indeed invent new forms of them; particularly since these have been discovered to be such rich sources of profit. For instance, human isolation is, in one sense, an existential affliction. It is experienced in even the most solidaristic societies by those whose personalities do not fit happily into the received social mould. But a different order of loneliness is produced by a society which 'cherishes' its individuals to such a degree that their own uniqueness becomes a major obstacle in understanding or sharing with anyone else.

The apologists of capitalism (actually they apologise no longer, but assert rather loudly) insist nevertheless that there is no connection between private moral failings and the energies which drive forward the economic system. It is clear that the vaunted transfiguration of human nature operates only in the economic arena; and indeed, when we look there, what we see is a vast increase in wealth. This dazzling reality is the tangible outcome, the crowning glory, of the subterranean operations of the system. The abundance of the West not only distracts our attention from the vast reservoirs of private misery which lie beneath its showy surface, but it is also used to reconcile us to the disfigurings that occur in society, where everything is supposed to embody the best of all possible words. In spite of the way in which our social life is dominated by the advertisers' hymns of praise and the publicists' sacred songs, these can scarcely disguise the prominence of fraud, speculation, theft, swindling, bribery, venality and corruption. In order to compensate both for the personal pain and the social scarrings, our private enjoyment of goods and services must be of such intensity as to keep us constantly in a state bordering on the ecstatic.

When they say 'You cannot change human nature', what they mean is 'We have unlocked the secret of wealth, and nothing must be permitted to change that'. For any change that interferes with the way that humanity is caught up in the process of wealth creation threatens that wealth itself. Thus, 'You cannot change human nature' is a symbolic statement about the precise way in which humanity is trapped in the machine. For the truth is that you can't 'change human nature' until human beings are disentangled from the machinery in which they are held fast. This human nature is not static, but imprisoned. Its immobility is indispensable to the dynamism of the system. It is, in fact, the one stable element which an unstable system requires.

This human nature, then, turns out to be nothing more than another prefabrication, a material far from raw. It has already been denatured before it ever appears on the stage of economic endeavour. There is nothing natural about this human nature. It has already been processed, selectively reshaped, so that what appear as inherent characteristics are merely an artefact, but one that is essential to justify the workings of the only permissible economic system.

This artificial human nature is then held up, not only as a true model of how people are, but also to show us what is required of us so that the system might not perish. There is, as they say in the movies, a very ugly word to describe the form of co-operation that is exacted by capitalism from its nominal beneficiaries. It is indeed a form of blackmail; one which threatens that any serious failure to live up to (or is it down to) a capitalist version of human nature, may result in the disappearance of the wealth that is its most conspicuous adornment.

In other words, if we do not agree absolutely with our blackmailers in their definition of our human nature, the goodies are liable to be snatched away without warning. The delicate balance of this imposed settlement gives cause for both anger and rejoicing; anger, because it represents the imposition upon us of a brutal and one-sided contract, which violates the very human nature in whose name it is promulgated; rejoicing, because this suggests that the whole edifice of an unyielding and immoveable status quo actually rests on more shaky foundations than all the pompous certainties about 'our human nature' would suggest. Our demeaning dependency upon the continuation of our apparent good fortune is as nothing compared to the dependency of our masters upon our unquestioning assent to their version of our shared, shabby and sordid nature.

Why ever should we dream of calling into question the profitable rigidity of this human nature, which has over the centuries shown itself to be capable of such prodigies of wealth creation? One good reason is that its earlier claim that it could deliver people from the age-old burdens of insecurity, want and fear once seemed plausible. At an earlier, possibly more innocent period, such pretensions had not yet been disconfirmed by the survival of these evils, and the growth of others alongside them. It is pertinent to ask how long economic growth of this kind must go on, when after more than two hundred years of promises that it would eliminate poverty, insecurity and need, these things have triumphantly survived all the wealth-creating capacities it has commanded.

What has now become plain is that economic growth has been, and remains, a substitute for universal sufficiency and human satisfactions, the ruin of which has been its most spectacular and lasting achievement. A humanity which has accepted this continuing growth and expansion as a surrogate for its own maturing and development is bound to have been radically falsified by such violence. Is it any wonder that it can no longer distinguish its own true nature from that caricature which has been imposed upon it?

13

NATURE

THE DISTORTIONS GO further; indeed, they comprehend the whole world. The maintenance of the system requires our inability to see clearly, not only our inner selves, but also the outer world of nature.

How easily we assimilate the social order with the natural order. The law of the jungle, the rat race, dog eat dog, red in tooth and claw, making a killing, going for the jugular, the killer instinct, baying for blood – how the common-sense imagery encapsulates what we take to be the fundamental law of evolution, the survival of the fittest.

In this account of the natural world and society, nature is exploited twice over. Nature is invoked in a set of false images which are then employed to support a tendentious version of human nature. Thus the world of nature, as represented in Christian cosmology, and taken to extremes by its bastard offspring, capitalism, is a place where the beasts tear each other apart, driven by blind instinct, rage, cruelty and predatory violence. Nature itself is dark, omnivorous, without pity, all teeth and ravening appetite; blood is the emblem of its remorseless vitality. To venture into such a savage terrain was a nightmare, to be borne only by those courageous, heroic individuals who opened up dark continents and forbidden territories, braving the poisoned arrows and lethal blowpipes of shadowy peoples who were themselves little more than an expression of the vicious and sombre forces that dominated a dangerous tropical habitat.

These images remain in spite of the revisions of Western environmentalists, and a vast media outpouring that has

126

transformed nature for a younger generation. Now it is full of exotic and threatened species which cry out for our protection; which is yet another strange mutation of the mission of the West and its dominion over nature. Yet the older imagery from a more directly colonial era with its bloody associations retains its power and co-exists with a more benign representation. The more violent view of nature has persisted because it is still functional, not so much in our apprehension of the natural world as in its serviceable purpose in accounting for the way we humans live and have to live. Even if nature does turn out to bear only the flimsiest resemblance to the gruesome projections of its industrial conquerors, this is likely to be rejected by a system which has constructed itself upon a fictitious real world, both human and natural.

The ideological importance and cultural centrality of our animal fables is perhaps best exemplified by our treatment of the wolf. It was Hobbes who articulated most forcefully the belief system which was to underpin political economy. At the heart of his sense of the cruelty and violence of social life lay a deeply pessimistic view of human nature which, in turn, rested upon his warped account of the animal world. He argues that natural society is 'the war of each against all', precisely because he believes that 'man is a wolf unto men' (*Homo homini lupus est*).

And indeed the wolf has been one of the most prominent predators in humanity's imagined bestiary, and no subsequent rehabilitation of the maligned wolf has changed its function in the social parables of the West. After all, are we not admonished to beware of wolves in sheep's clothing, because they are inwardly ravening? Red Riding Hood was punished for her failure to distinguish between the wolf and her close kin. Only the little pig prudent enough to build his house of bricks found it could withstand the violently destructive breath of the fierce wolf. Is it not an irony that one of the justifications for our heaping up of riches is 'to keep the wolf from the door', long after the unhappy creature has disappeared from the domesticated landscapes of Western Europe? To cry wolf means falsely signalling disaster and danger, and thereby exposing innocents to the sudden savagery of its attack. Appetites, both for food and sex, are described as 'wolfish'. Is not the werewolf the incarnation of the darkest impulses in human beings? The wolf is always ready to descend on the fold, and leave a trail of havoc and blood. Is not the lone wolf – our symbol for the unsocialised, the outcast, the psychopath – even more dangerous than the wolves who customarily hunt in the dense grey mass of the pack?

Poor wolf. Of course, wolves were once a threat to human beings, but only in the way that human beings have always been a threat to all other animals, and are now threatening to extinguish them completely. It has to be said that there is no record of a pack of wolves having imprisoned human beings for their own entertainment, nor of having hunted them down for sport or pleasure.

Whether or not our cultural heritage embodies an accurate picture of the wolf is more than a matter for academic debate – it is crucial. Just suppose we were to discover that wolves are altogether different from our images of them. What if they were found to be sociable creatures, with elaborate social structures based upon kinship, with a respect for each other and for those species which they do not need for nourishment, with a particular aversion to damaging the weaker members of their own pack, and with highly developed instincts of solidarity? Would we then be prepared to feel differently about the wolf? And, more to the point, would we come to feel differently about ourselves?

Perhaps it is more convenient to cling to our stories of the big, bad wolf, to the fairy tales of our culture, to the fables of our political economy. We may wonder whose interests these falsehoods serve. Clearly not those of the wolf; nor even of those humans who might wish to create a different relationship with wolves than one governed by fear, hatred and contempt. Those advantaged by the traditional version of the wolf are those who profit from all those actions which have been called 'wolfish' in 'human' nature. If the wolf continues to prowl hungrily, it does so, not in the lonely reaches of the frozen pine forest, but in the mysterious thickets of the human psyche.

If the wolf, that archetype of ferocious cruelty and unre-
strained appetite can be so untrue to its nature, we may well
wonder what other symbols, stereotypes and certainties are
equally unreliable. We might imagine that it was the lived
reality of our interaction with wolves which etched our
knowledge of their nature so clearly upon our folk memory.
Yet even when we had direct contact with wolves, this did
not stop us from projecting upon them something which we
did not wish to acknowledge about ourselves. This was
nothing other than that aspect of our nature for which, in
those less enlightened times, we still felt obliged to discover
an alibi. We wanted to cast out those human characteristics
which disturbed our serenity, and the unfortunate wolf was
well placed to receive the full force of our repudiated self-
knowledge. Now that so few of us ever encounter wolves,
how much easier it has become for us to see the presence of
imagined wolfishness in our fellow human beings. The animals have gone, but the bestiary remains. The after-image of
the fallen jungle lingers on, with its rapacity, and competitive
struggles, with the weakest being continually trampled under-
foot. The imagery continues to nourish our popular conception of humanity: the popular press now habitually refers to
wrong-doers in terms of 'beasts', 'brutes', 'animals',
'inhuman monsters'.

None of this is to deny that there is a kind of 'beast within',
but it has nothing to do with animals, other than those of
the human kind. All societies provide ample evidence of a
human capacity for cruelty, for atrocities against each other,
which no other animal has ever had the ingenuity to invent.
Indeed, these are the very forces which capitalism claims to
keep in check by permitting them to go about their work
only under licence, under the authorisation of economic
forces. These then do for us in the world what we would still
be ashamed to do for ourselves. When the laws of the market
oppress or maim or kill, no human agency is involved, no
responsibility is conceded. If these forces of aggression appear
more autonomous, this is because they are conceived of as
impersonal, beyond human control, so unlike that more familiar violence which expresses itself in murderous hand-to-

hand combat or that lays waste cities and cornfields by fire and by sword, or by the deployment of smart weapons in hi-tech TV wars. If the Western system really could transform the ferocious energies of human beings into a benign force that merely creates wealth, then it would indeed have worked wonders.

Whether capitalism has any such powers may best be judged by the way in which it has despoiled the planet and violated its peoples. Rather than having tamed 'the beast in man', capitalism has excited and inflamed its passions. It is a far cry from the comfortingly domestic imagery of Adam Smith, with his private interests of the butcher and the baker, to the private interests of Unilever, Shell or Mitsubishi, whose self-interest may or may not provide us with our dinner, but whose workings certainly do provide for us those images of mono-cultural plantations of oil palm, charred stumps of forest trees, flocks of seabirds tarred by spillages, and environmental refugees driven from subsistence farms into rows of flimsy canvas on the edges of Third World cities. The sentimental belief that private vice can be so easily trans-formed into public good has permitted precisely the opposite to occur: private vice now appears in the world as public viciousness under the logos of transnational companies.

Just as the wolf is the characteristic creature of our dis-torted nature, so the jungle is the emblematic habitat of that nature. When we hear that we have no choice but to defer to the 'laws of the jungle' in the way we live with each other, we should be doubly wary; firstly because it is always wrong to use nature to legitimate social arrangements, and secondly because the view of the jungle presented is unlikely to have any but the most tenuous connection with the real laws of the actual jungle.

In Western iconography, the jungle is a place of seething life, exotic and threatening. Jungles are what intrepid explorers disappear into. It is a living, greedy, blood-red orifice; a treacherous female luring men to seductive deaths. It is a place of myriad life-forms, a slithering sinuousity of strange creatures, their vibrant colours muted by impassable thickets. It is a place of deception, where sticks turn into

snakes and creatures drop out of the trees; of eerie screech-
ings and chatterings, a sub-human speech, also uttered by
the scarcely human kin of the monkeys, who grub up roots
for their sustenance and make their dress of tree bark. Here
is chaos, all that is the opposite of civilisation, reason and
order. The smell is of decay, of things that have blossomed
and faded in a day. Everything is out of control, and the
sickly sweetness of death hovers on the air. The beauty of
the jungle is tainted by the presence of dangerous insects;
spiders and poisonous creatures emerge from the flawless
flowers. It is oppressive and airless; languorous butterflies,
sulphur-yellow and crimson, wheel over the fleshy proboscis
of nameless plants; only the whiteness of bared teeth shines
in the darkness. The jungle is savage, remorseless, without
pity. Its paths lead nowhere, or only into hidden danger.
Behind the animal predators lurk painted savages, with poisoned darts aimed at the explorers who have come to bring
them into the clear light of civilisation.

The jungle, however, is not a general version of nature,
but is an image which occurs because of a specific historical
and political relationship between the West and the places
where jungle landscapes are found. We can see the particu-
larity of this imaging if we compare it with the role of the
forest in popular perception.

The forest is more familiar, the product of more temperate
climates, and its mysteries are manageable. The forest also
formerly held its dangers but it also offered shelter for those
compelled to take refuge from the arbitrariness of feudal rule.
It was not an inhospitable place, for here Robin Hood was
able to carry out his rudimentary practice of social justice,
long before the wise legislators of England had established it
more definitively. The forest is also a place for hunting; not
the hunt after tigers, lions, elephants and other ferocious
creatures, but the more stately pursuit of the deer. It is the
habitat of the sturdy English oak; its clearings are patches of
sunlight, where the people compete in friendly tournaments,
jousting and archery, and feast off fine English beef and
venison.

But the forest is more than this. It is also a retreat, where

131

hermits contemplate and gather wisdom, and it offered the opportunity for solitude, for escape from an extending civilisation. It is a site of shrines, pilgrimages, holy places, where self-knowledge may be sought; it is the *selva oscura* of Dante's beginning of a journey of enlightenment. Forests were magical, too, the settings of fairy tales, of castles around which the briars grew, where animals spoke and heroes gathered their strength for the coming battle. They were meeting places for beasts with humans, where those who knew how to listen might learn the wisdom of the owl, the cunning of the fox, the swiftness of the hare and the strength of bear. Nature gave freely of her bounty in the forest; there were nuts and wild raspberries, blackberries and mushrooms, in contrast to the lurid and often poisonous harvest of the jungle. Here, Mother Nature reigns, whereas the destructive Kali holds the jungle under her sway. We can understand the forest; we feel at home there, whereas we are always strangers in that inhospitable, alien jungle which must remain forever closed upon its menacing secrets.

No doubt we would never have forsaken the familiarity of the forest for the certain risks and doubtful prizes of the jungle, had we not been compelled to do so, and by our own actions. We were exiled from the English forest paradise because we had destroyed it. After all, by the 1820s, only one twenty-third of the land surface of Britain was still covered with forest; whereas a century earlier, it had still been one-sixth. Ecological ruin was a major factor which impelled our jungle expeditions and tropical discoveries. Not only had we exhausted the supply of hearty English oak to build ships for trade and war, but we had also discovered that the teaks of Malabar were more durable in naval construction than the sturdiest of our native trees. In other words, it was because we had used up *our* forests that we had to come to terms with *their* jungles; even though the terms on which we did this remained ours.

The heroics of those expeditions have been much exaggerated. The harsh picture of the jungle which became part of our culture comes from our lack of familiarity with it. We had no living relationship with the jungle; nor did we intend to develop one. Is our image of the jungle as a place of savagery, violence and cruelty merely a reflection of our desire to demolish it, to reduce it to mere wood and timber? Do we always have to make savage that which we intend to destroy? And what can our attachment to our own beloved landscapes, our forests and woodlands mean, when we so wholeheartedly set about their annihilation? We may see in our sentimental destructiveness a different kind of pathetic fallacy than that attributed to the Romantic poets, who saw in the forests a source of moral instruction, and a mirror of changing feelings. Is our tenderness for the ruined landscapes, our concern, in a more contemporary idiom, for the environment, nostalgia, hypocrisy or remorse? If we see the jungle as primitive and cruel, this is because we intend to destroy it; if we see the forest as sylvan and vernal, this is because we have destroyed it already. It used to be said of those who lacked clarity of vision that they could not see the wood for the trees; our special failing is that we are unable to discern the trees at all, because our eyes can see only the commercial value of the timber.

No wonder we still need the image of the jungle in these urban societies which now occupy the sites of vanished forests. This false image of the jungle has now been transferred to something we call 'the urban jungle', where it is exploited to explain and justify even more predatory treatment of one another.

These consistent misperceptions are shown up as the crude caricatures they are, when we listen to the people of the jungle. They have quite other stories, and the feelings which arise from their symbiosis with the jungle are very different. Not only is their view based more closely on daily familiarity with their habitat, but even their projections and imaginings serve to preserve their own way of life and the life of the jungle. Whatever gods, spirits or demons inhabit these settings, these are nevertheless allies in the work of preservation, and their modes of worship – what used to be called by Christian explorers 'mumbo-jumbo' – ensure that the jungle and everything it shelters are treated reverentially, and used only sparingly, economically (if this word can still be employed to indicate restraint).

It is difficult for us to imagine how a knowledge of the jungle can create such powerful positive feelings, such love, when in our own cosmology, the jungle serves such eccentric fantasies. Jungle voices are rarely heard, except as examples of aberrant cultural practices and bizarre customs.

This is how Winin Pereira describes a young woman of the Warli tribal people of Northern Maharashtra in India:

> Raji Vavre, a twelve-year-old, knows the names of over a hundred herbs, shrubs and trees, and their varied uses. Many of these supplement her basic diet of cereals and pulses with essential proteins, vitamins and minerals. She knows which plants are a source of fibre, which are good for fuel and lighting, which have medical uses. She knows how to get crabs out of their holes, and to trap fish. She can catch wild hare, quail and partridges, and locate birds' nests.[21]

The Lumad of the Philippines, speaking of their traditional farming practice in the forested hills of Mindanao say:

> Through *kaingin*, the trees are cut but the seedlings are left to grow again. When the area begins to be revegetated, a baby forest, the growth of trees after slash and burn, is created.
>
> Underneath the forests are seeds and seedlings that grow with enough sunlight. The passing of time will, definitely, not alter nature's way. While there is a tree, there is a seed, and while there is a seed and the sun, there is the forest.
>
> Doing kaingin stems from the authority accorded to Magba-baya; in the event of a bad omen, or *bagtu*, after asking the permission of the spirit, the plan to do kaingin is not pushed through. Practising kaingin is anchored in assuring that no damage is done to adjoining parcels of land; holy and sacred places are excluded; the shifting nature of kaingin ensures that the forest is preserved and the fertility of the soil maintained. The Lumad believe that all things and creatures that grow on the earth have, in one way or another, special relations to their life and culture. Thus all yield and produce are not for individual consumption alone, but are shared with the *Tagbaya* (gods or spirits) and all other creatures.[20]

Survival International has been working for a quarter of

a century for the rights of indigenous peoples all over the world, and has defended them against the encroachments of alien economic interests. Its report on the Yanomami in Brazil's rainforest gives us a glimpse of their response to the jungle:

> For the Yanomami, the world of everyday life is part of the larger spirit world, which they treat in the same way as they do one another. Thus, when they garden or gather or hunt, taking from nature, they are incurring a debt, arousing the vengeful spirits of dead plants and animals. These attack the Yanomami in their dreams, and are said to account for much illness. They can only be controlled by special song and dance, by shamans which bring the aid of 'helpers' from among the creator spirits . . . Such wariness of nature is perhaps typical of many aboriginal peoples. In the Yanomami's case it serves to express a sense of deep practical and emotional attachment to the forest which is their home.[23]

These accounts of another relationship with the jungle show us more clearly how we falsify it for our own purposes. We project ideas, feelings and ideologies on to nature, which are emanations, not only of our social structures, but also of the unresolved, and indeed unresolvable conflicts of our existence. These all flow into one another, mix and harden to create what becomes the fundamental beliefs of our culture. Might it be possible to isolate the different elements in this ideology, and reassemble them in another combination? Were we able to do so, we might then be able to distinguish what can be changed in our lives from what cannot be changed; and also, how what cannot be changed might be made more bearable by drawing on the only resource that we have, which remains a recognition of our shared fate on earth.

14

THE NATURE OF OUR LIVES

IT IS, OF course, almost impossible to take to pieces an ideology in which we must live and which lives through us; particularly one which is so powerful, and which appears to reconcile within itself all existing contradictions.

Thus, if nature is seen essentially as 'red in tooth and claw' this 'unalterable' fact is used to reinforce the equally fundamental rapacity of human nature. This aspect of nature's violence justifies wresting from it such treasures as heroic human beings may win in their conquest of nature. The West's celebrated 'conquest of nature' is, however, at best very partial. It is not able to subdue the bestiality of the animals; but it can kill them. It is not able to live in the jungle, but it can destroy all the trees in them. Conquest means not overcoming (whatever that might mean), but exploiting. Similarly, of course, human nature can never be changed, but it can be conquered to the extent that it can also be exploited by its passage through the mysterious distilleries of wealth creation, and emerge on the other side, harmless, domesticated, tractable.

But a resourceful Western world view also makes available an alternative version of nature. This is nature as the restorer, the consoler, and even the instructor. It is essential for ideologies which have pretensions to stability and universality that they should appear to contain within themselves key incompatibilities and irreconcilables. In this subordinate narrative within the ideology, nature provides refreshment for the jaded spirit, gives strength to carry on, and its grandeur serves to remind us of the pettiness of the daily struggle. We catch a glimpse of the relative unimportance of our efforts when we stand in the presence of the eternal mountains and the ever-changing skies. Nature, and its ally, time, are the great healers, the assuagers of loss. Nature, as the symbol of renewal, is also the pledge of restoration, of separations overcome; we comfort ourselves by planting evergreens in our graveyards.

Some have seen nature as an even more specific source of instruction. Wordsworth, who is still seen as the great worshipper of nature, bids us listen to it:

> And hark! how blithe the throstle sings!
> He, too, is no mean preacher:
> Come forth into the light of things,
> Let Nature be your Teacher.[24]

From the Romantic movement onwards, nature became a conductor for decayed religious feeling, and people often said that they could worship their creator better among the hills than they could in cramped brick preaching houses. Nature had traditionally been seen in Christian teaching as the other book in which the Creator had revealed something of Himself. As faith in the more orthodox text dwindled, at least the book of nature remained to lift up the hearts of a toiling industrial proletariat. Indeed, it became the mission of many who sought to rescue an urbanised and corrupted people to bring them once more within sight of the beneficent and civilising influence of green fields; it was said of slum children, as the ultimate proof of their degraded sensibility, that they had never seen a cow.

The distant inheritor of this worship of nature has been the Green movement. In their over-reaction to the eager industrial conquest of nature, its exploitation and subjection, the Greens have seen nature as the ultimate source of moral values. What they call 'living in harmony with nature' is often taken to mean that there is some eternal order in nature, an order which we must imitate and not upset or alter in any particular. Such reverence for nature could be the product only of a highly urbanised society, one long out of contact with that respect for nature which peasant societies were compelled to observe. It is the distinction between 'sacred earth' and 'pig earth'. Those who depended upon the earth for immediate survival never sentimentalised it, for it required great effort to win a livelihood from it. The idea of nature as 'holy' is potentially as damaging as the industrial world view which sees nature as nothing more than inert 'raw materials'. It is damaging because this form of worship of the natural world leads so easily to seeing human beings as its only despoilers, as parasitic upon it. It is then only a small step to a greenery so deep that it would see the people perish rather than one eco-system disturbed. Agriculture itself has always involved a deep disruption of the natural world, yet few would wish to abandon it on the grounds that it interferes with nature. What we can say is that human creativity allied to a respect for all living and growing things is a different sensibility, both from the destructiveness which sees nature as its enemy, and which would tear from it its living heart, and from a worship that sees nature as inviolable.

We cannot draw moral lessons from nature. The sounds we hear are echoes of our own voices; the signs we read are the shadows of our inscriptions. Nature is not red in tooth and claw; nor does it embody a moral code for humanity. Yet our interdependence with nature is fundamental. The connectedness between human beings and all living (and non-living) elements of nature does offer instruction on how we need to behave towards the natural world. It is our failure to understand the dynamics of this relationship which has led us to our present predicament. It seems we always abuse nature, in one mode or another, by projecting on to its enduring indifference our own moods and purposes. The best we can do is rescue nature from all ideology, that we may perceive our own destiny more clearly as part of its workings. We cannot draw moral lessons, but there is still something to be learned.

As with nature, so with human nature. Here, the dominant view of our competitive, selfish, unalterable nature is very clear. How quickly the two natures come together, as we press our barnyard imagery on to human affairs. Everyone wants to feather his own nest, to be top dog, to rule the roost, to stand high in the pecking order, to crow over his success, to claw his way to the top, to get his snout in the trough, to live like a pig in clover. But here we find again an accommodating dualism. It is also in our nature to give a helping hand, to see ourselves in the sufferings of others, to protect your own kin, to look after your own, to feel for your nearest and dearest. 'It's only natural' can cover a wide range of human conduct; maternal instincts, brotherly love, helping your neighbour, falling in love. But what is natural in these benign responses also has a sting in the tail; for its corollary in what is not natural, shows its limits. 'It's not natural', for instance for two men or two women to love one another; 'it's not natural' to concern yourself over-much with suffering in remote parts of the world (charity always begins at home). 'It's not natural' to betray your country, no matter how malign its work in the world may be.

The idea that human nature is 'fundamentally' either one thing or the other is the real problem. All that we can say is that human nature is indeed ambiguous, capable of both great good and great evil. But this is a comfortable truism. What is critical is our response to these ambiguities, these dividednesses. The greatest damage inflicted by the social and economic system of the West comes from its promise that it will spare us having to face these contradictions and necessary tensions. Because we continue to believe that evil can be released into an economic system, and emerge mysteriously transformed into good, we are prevented from addressing the real ambiguities of human nature. This abridges discussion about how a social order might mitigate our undoubted power for evil as well as enhance our equally real potential for kindness.

This is how the way we live comes to appear 'natural', and therefore unchallengeable; we, not the unfortunate indigenous peoples, are the ones who are truly living in a state of nature. For what could be more natural than that our social structures should reflect both (our view of) the natural world and (our perception of) human nature? If our social arrangements are based upon competition and selfishness, this is quite simply because these are the dominant characteristics of both the natural and the human world. It is true that there are spaces, protected environments, in which human beings may indulge their taste for kindness and caring; human nature reserves, as it were, where happy families may picnic, untroubled by the wild beasts of greed and avarice that prowl outside the reinforced rustic fence.

This is the true basis on which the final apotheosis, the last triumphal stage of an uncontested global capitalism, is built. This social system, unlike any other, is the true reflection of the natural order. Here we see the supreme resolution of humanity with nature; and the highest wisdom of humanity lies in assent to this happy state. Our civilisation has at last obeyed the original philosophic injunction; we have come to know ourselves, and further, we have constructed a social system which perfectly articulates that knowledge. This is how the world is, and anyone who would disturb such harmony and serenity could be animated only by a diabolic wickedness. Whenever people raise their voices in protest against some further imposition, or some further sacrifice demanded by the system, they are silenced, not by the refusal of the most benign of systems to grant their wishes, but by the verdict of that final court of appeal, the laws of nature. If the system should appear cruel, it is merely acting under higher instruction, and its very cruelties are evidence of its authenticity.

These interpretations of the world take their ultimate strength from an inescapable apprehension that life itself is fundamentally cruel. It is from exploiting this incontestable truth that our social structures derive their final plausibility. We all know that our lives are subject to loss and suffering, to separation and decay, to sickness and death. It is left to our poets to proclaim that life's joys are short-lived, pleasure fleeting, that nothing endures. We know this all too well. The passage of time brings degradation, infirmity, loss of beauty and the shrivelling of possibilities. And, in the end, such afflictions are irremediable, even if not unassuagable.

We find it hard to come to terms with our inevitable human fate, because in the end, there can be no adequate response to it. Faced with the impossibility of any rational way of dealing with these intractable experiences, is it any wonder that faith fills the space where our incomprehension cannot rest? Unhappily, faith is no more capable of rest than is incomprehension. It will always return to the world in the guise of knowledge, certainty, even revelation. If only faith could remain, as it has sometimes been represented, a flickering, a mobile intermittent tingeing of the darkness, rather than the blinding light it invariably becomes.

If we so easily tolerate the grievous inequalities of social systems, this is because life itself, we know, is not fair. We know that suffering is unequally distributed, like beauty or wit. Some people have more than their share of pain (a homely phrase, sadly indicative of our recognition of profound 'natural' injustices); others get away with murder and sleep soundly in their beds. We may console ourselves with a belief in the existence of hidden compensatory mechanisms, whereby the most fortunate are not always happy, or even the most wretched outcast enjoys consolations unseen. For millions of beings who come into the world, the light glimmers for a moment and is gone; women give birth bestride a grave. There is no justice.

Here is the fundamental reason why people treat each other so badly, no matter under what social and economic orderings they live. We are all abused children, injured by the longing for permanence, stability and continuity, whereas our experience is all of separation, dissolution and disruption. We have all been orphaned by existence, no matter how solicitous our nurturing may have been. We have cause to be angry, sad and bitter.

However, we soon realise that there are no satisfactory outlets for our anger and bitterness. We may trouble deaf heaven with our bootless cries, rend our garments, even curse the day we were born, but the heavens give little sign of responding. We inflict no apparent injury upon them, however vehement our outpourings. So, what could be more natural, what could be more human, than that we should vent our dissatisfactions and the furies they engender within us, where they can be effective; upon other creatures that are, fortunately, sentient? Our feeling of the fundamental wrong that has been done to us finds its most tangible expression in the wrongs we do to others.

Such responses are common to all societies. Ruth Benedict describes how the Kwakiutl deal with death and bereavement:

> When a chief's son died, the chief set out in his canoe. He was received at the house of a neighbouring chief, and after the formalities, he addressed his host, saying 'My prince has died today, and you go with him.' Then he killed him. In this, according to their interpretation, he acted nobly, because he had not been downed, but had struck back in return.
>
> There are many stories of this behaviour at death. A chief's sister and her daughter had gone up to Victoria, and, either because they drank bad whisky or because their boat capsized, they never came back. The chief called together his warriors. 'Now I ask you, tribes, who shall wail? Shall I do it, or shall another?' The spokesman answered, of course: 'Not you, chief. Let some other of the tribes.' Immediately, they set up the war pole, to announce their intention of wiping out the injury and gathered a war party. They set out and found seven men and two children asleep and killed them. Then they felt good when they arrived at Sebaa in the evening.[25]

Our first reaction to this story is 'How strange. What incomprehensible behaviour.' But a little reflection reveals that it is but a more explicit rendering of our own response to loss. For the satisfaction of making others suffer along with us is accompanied by a wonderful accession of power. We might even argue that our own society is more cruel, for we embark upon such pre-emptive retaliation without even waiting for the proximate cause that drives the logic of the Kwakiutl. When we cause others to grieve, whatever the apparatus of legitimation we may work through – the just war, the good cause, economic necessity, reasons of state – we become majestic, assimilated to those blind forces of nature which themselves work their worst upon us, and to which we owe a life. At such times, we feel that we are at one with the powers of the universe, at one with nature, mighty, invulnerable, on the side of the eternal victor. We become as mysterious as death, as impalpable as suffering, as untouchable as pain. We become someone else's destiny. General Norman Schwarzkopf, US Forces Commander in the Gulf, urged his men into battle on 17 January 1991 with these words: 'Our cause is just. Now you must be the thunder and lightning of Desert Storm.' Our cause is always just. Our exultation in the pain of others is always dissimulated behind the mask of the righteous, as we see the tyrant humbled, the adversary brought low, the evil-doer punished. Those upon whom we visit our anger, whatever injuries they may have inflicted upon us, stand also in place of the ghostly perpetrators of far deeper woundings.

Societies that take inspiration from such unanswerable truths of nature can plausibly deny that they are mere social systems. They draw their strength from a kind of honesty, a form of integrity in their demand for acceptance of the necessary cruelties of a system that is now indistinguishable from life itself. The naturalisation of society is accomplished. How flimsy by comparison are aspirations to 'change things'.

The full force of this structure of feeling lay behind much of the 'conservative' politics that has swept the world since the Eighties. The Right has been able to glory in a brutal radicalism. Their lips have been unsealed after the long years of discretion forced upon them by welfarism and the attenuated ideologies of concern. The Right can now reaffirm fundamental truths, basic realities, the way things are. They do not flinch now from presenting us with the strange mendacities of their home truths; they come as liberators, as bringers of a breath of fresh air, as escape from the straitjacket of collectivism and control. They exposed the hollow claims of those who had declared that you can make people good, indeed that you can change them, by a modest amelioration of their environment. Well, they said, the environment has been changed, improved beyond all recognition, but people remain as selfish and greedy as they ever were. Nor is this something to be ashamed of. Selfishness and greed are the greatest promoters of human betterment. The last decade has felt like an object lesson in the folly of seeking to make changes which go against the laws, not merely of a social system, but of the universe, of which that system is a true reflection. Those who still speak of modifying the worst effects of the existing order by intervening in its mysterious workings now stand revealed as credulous at best, at worst, wicked. For they are seeking to go against nature.

It cannot be denied that life is often violently deceptive, cruelly disappointing and radically unsatisfying. There is, however, more than one way of responding to this reality. Nothing on earth compels us to imitate it, to mimic its cruelty, to replicate its harshness. Above all, we do not have to assent to a system which extends, legitimates, and even glories in such disagreeable truths. No higher authority compels us to identify ourselves with those forces of nature whose victims all of us will, sooner or later, become.

Many argue that it is only 'natural' for us to ally ourselves with what appears strong, invincible, all-powerful in the world. Tyrants have never lacked their flatterers and supporters, those who uphold their right to rage against the weak, the unprotected, the vulnerable. Because death always wins, we are drawn to identify ourselves with those whose provisional victories over other people offer us a sense of privileged proximity to these awesome forces.

Nevertheless the West has always claimed, as one of its distinctive contributions to civilisation, that human beings are capable of distinguishing themselves from the blind and destructive forces of nature, precisely by the use of reason and reflection. It is this appeal to the supremacy of reason that is the crowning glory of the Western tradition. The historical record suggests, however, that the actual behaviour of Western societies scarcely sustains this high claim. Indeed, its behaviour in the world exhibits all too close a kinship with that of all other societies. There is nothing special about the West. Where it has had the power and strength, it has not forborne to use them in the most violent and coercive manner; in the conquest of the weak, the subordination of other societies, and the imposition of its values, for which it claims universal validity. Its own justification for this proselytising endeavour has been precisely that it represents the highest domination of nature through its technology, and the truest reflection of nature in its social and moral structures.

Western society has had the good fortune, vouchsafed to no other on earth, to have been virtually unchecked in its expansion across the globe. This has only served to confirm its deeply held belief in its own superiority, and in the uniqueness of its own access to truth. Unhappily, in this respect, it only betrays its similarity with all other functioning human societies, who have seen their value systems as a representation of how things eternally are, and therefore must be.

Of course, all societies, however monolithic their belief systems, produce heretics, groups of dissidents, who perceive the arbitrariness of the prevailing ideology. This permits them to see the cruel folly of compelling others to observances which have only local validity, even to the extent of killing those who will not believe. Such dissenters may then go on to construct an alternative, but equally totalising picture of the world; or, in the space that has been opened up by their own unbelief, they may come to doubt the existence of absolute truths. Such people are unlikely to want to kill for the sake of these perceptions. The more difficult question, however, is whether any effective society could base itself on such a modest vision of the world; or whether its own self-reflective qualities would not lead to its disintegration, or to its being swept aside by other, more confident societies. Is it possible for a society to exist without an ideology? It is not sufficient that, like the West, a society should hide its ideology by disowning the one that animates it. Indeed, the very invisibility of the ideology of the West to its people poses the greatest danger, both to the West itself and to the rest of the world, however valuable this concealment might be for its own internal cohesion. This invisibility of the dogmas of the West permit the elaboration of a bogus pluralism, a specious diversity, and spurious freedoms of choice.

If all societies end up spreading death and suffering in the interests of self-preservation and expansion, then there can be little to say in the presence of this bleakest view of human destiny. But if this does not have to be so, what can we do to help our own society to be otherwise?

The strength and power of what are, after all, only ideologies, comes from the suppressed knowledge of the unsatisfactoriness of the unalterable circumstances in which we must live and die. Perhaps our most useful work in the world is to begin to distinguish between the irremediable and that which can be remedied; to exhume the existential skeleton from the ideological grave; or, should we rather not say, to exhume the ideological skeleton from where it has long lain, in the existential grave? Is it our fear of corpses, or of death itself, or a reluctance to disturb the sleep of the dead, that makes us so unwilling to seek the human remains amid so much ideological putrefaction?

In other words, if only we were able to separate the conditions of our existence from ideological responses to them, we might then be free to imagine other ways of dealing with what is truly unalterable.

This making of clear distinctions in our view of nature is a most fundamental task. Those who deplore human disharmony with nature, and our estrangement from it, have only part of the picture; just as those who insist that the whole of nature is there to be conquered (except invincible human nature), are similarly partial in their view. We need to enrich and balance these one-sided accounts of the world, and to rebuild our relationship with it. We need to identify with the eternal cycle of replenishment and regeneration, but to avoid identifying ourselves with nature as the agent of death and destruction.

There is a strong case to be made for resisting with all our energy those who would seize themselves of nature's purpose, those who would add to the burden of suffering that awaits us all. If there is a crucial difference between human beings and the rest of the natural world (and, in spite of some deep Green philosophies, there is), it lies precisely in our powers to resist, or at least not to augment, the cruelties that none can escape. Our supreme distinction lies in our capacity to mitigate human suffering; for nothing else in the world can do so. This distinction between ourselves and the rest of creation is, in fact, one of the greatest resources we have; and this is a distinction which deserves more attention than many other proud claims to human singularity.

But what is to stop us from looking upon the most baleful

aspects of nature, and simply assimilating ourselves to them? Why should we choose to resist an alliance with the blind destructive forces of nature, when it is so much easier not to?

If we refuse to become like death, nature's unappealable last judgement, then at least we resist becoming accessories to our own extinction, or indeed, to the extinction of others. If we do resist, we lessen the burden of suffering, and however small our contribution, we shall feel that we have had another kind of triumph over our fate, however partial, temporary or local. We can, of course, never finally win, but at least we shall not have furthered the work of ruin and loss in the world, for which the industrial mono-culture which we call our society is such an effective vehicle. Wherever we resist, we create spaces for such companionability and conviviality as may be possible; for we see each other's faces only by the light of the fires we kindle.

This may seem a thin argument set against the certainties of those who wield power over others, of those who spread desolation, who have usurped the necessities of the poor and carried off their booty to the high places of the world; of those who have lived in the serene enjoyment of the fruits of violence, who have died in comfort in the respect of their fellows after lives of tireless rapacity and unblemished selfishness. Can there be enough in a refusal to imitate them in their impersonation of death to move us to virtue?

After all, most other persuasions to goodness have had somewhat more showy rewards to offer. They felt bound to promise images of streets of jasper and gold, of celestial banquets, or of reclining on silken couches while favoured attendants brought goblets of honeyed sherbet; or of resting on Abraham's bosom, or walking in the fields of Elysium. If we eschew such glamorous offers, what inducements can we hold out for unrecompensed goodness, what can we promise to each other as the reward of virtue?

It may be that those who declare that rewards and incentives are required (at whatever level) to make people good, mistake the nature of such rewards, as they are to be had here on earth. Perhaps we cannot aim so high. We may not

147

be able to offer convincing reasons to be virtuous, but we can at last challenge the reasons that are advanced for being vicious. The apologia for the structures of cruelty and violence upon which our precarious and tainted well-being is founded, can be contested. This is the most we can do. And if we cannot see through the appearance of the world to a hidden moral order, at least we can turn round and see our likeness in the features of those who journey with us. If none can avoid the onward march of death and dissolution, at least we do not have to embrace them, or urge our companions into their arms.

Modest as these claims undoubtedly are, they do gain an added force from the extremity of the present time. The ideological distortions which we have imposed, both upon the ambiguities of nature and the dividedness of our own human nature, have brought us to a world strewn with the wreckage of a despoiled nature and a broken humanity. Our religious visions, as well as the secular dreams that replaced them both lie in material ruin. The wind howls around those who live in the last refuges of the painted pleasure gardens of the West. Death has many guises, and often appears masked. He comes to us in the colours of preternatural springtime, promising endless renewal, boundless hope and eternal youthfulness, even as he prepares to abandon us to the exhausted wastes of perpetual winter.

References

1 (p. 6) England Arise! Edward Carpenter 1886; cited Tony Benn, ed. Writing on the Wall, Faber 1984.
2 (p. 7) News from Nowhere, William Morris, Lawrence & Wishart, 1977.
3 (p. 15) Rural Rides, William Cobbett, Penguin ed. 1983.
4 (p. 24) Thomas Carlyle, Past and Present, Everyman ed., Dent 1960.
5 (p. 34) Friedrich Engels, The Condition of the Working Class in England in 1844, Allen & Unwin, 1952.
6 (p. 41) F. Engels, op. cit.
7 Henry Mayhew, London Labour and London Poor, Penguin 1985.
8 (p. 43) F. Engels, op. cit.
9 (p. 48) F. Engels, op. cit.
10 (p. 49) Jaya Jetly, The Economic Times, New Delhi, 27.4.92.
11 (p. 69) Dilwyn Jenkins, worker at Machynlleth, Alternative Technology Centre.
12 (p. 70) Helena Norberg-Hodge, quoted in Pioneers of Change, Jeremy Seabrook, Zed 1993. Helena Norberg-Hodge's book, Ancient Futures was published in 1992.
13 (p. 71) Coming of Age in Samoa, Margaret Mead, Penguin 1966.
14 (p. 74) We The Invisible, Society for the Promotion of Area Resource centres, 52 Miami Bhulabhai Desai Road, Bombay 400026, 1984.
15 (p. 88) Eric Williams, Capitalism and Slavery, Andre Deutsch, 1975.
16 (p. 91) Jeremy Seabrook, The Race for Riches, Marshall Pickering 1988.

17 (p. 98) Josinaldo Aleixo de Sousa, Rio de Janeiro, 1992.
18 (p. 103) Ruth Benedict, Patterns of Culture, Mentor, 1951.
19 (p. 108) George Eliot, Scenes from Clerical Life, Penguin 1976.
20 (p. 121) Adam Smith, The Wealth of Nations, Penguin ed 1982.
21 (p. 134) Asking the Earth, Winin Pereira and Jeremy Seabrook, Earthscan 1991.
22 (p. 134) Struggle Against Development Aggression, Tunay Na Alyansa Ng Bayan Alay Sa Katutubo (TABAK), Manila, The Philippines, 1990.
23 (p. 135) Survival International, Newsletter, 1992.
24 (p. 137) The Tables Turned, Works, William Wordsworth, OUP 1960.
25 (p. 142) Ruth Benedict, op. cit.